TOP
PERFORMER

Also by Stephen C. Lundin, Ph.D.

Fish! (with Harry Paul and John Christensen)
Fish! Tales (with Harry Paul, John Christensen
and Philip Strand)
Fish! Sticks (with Harry Paul and John Christensen)

**Stephen C. Lundin, Ph.D.
and Carr Hagerman, PSP**

TOP PERFORMER

A Bold Approach to Sales and Service

**HODDER
MOBIUS**

Copyright © 2007 by Stephen C. Lundin and Carr Hagerman

First published in Great Britain in 2007 by Hodder & Stoughton
A division of Hodder Headline

The right of Stephen C. Lundin and Carr Hagerman to be identified as the
Authors of the Work has been asserted by them in accordance with the
Copyright, Designs and Patents Act 1988.

A Mobius book

1

A CIP catalogue record for this title is available from the British Library

ISBN 978 0 340 92409 9
ISBN 0 340 92409 8

Printed and bound by Mackays of Chatham Ltd, Chatham, Kent

Hodder Headline's policy is to use papers that are natural,
renewable and recyclable products and made from wood grown
in sustainable forests. The logging and manufacturing processes are
expected to conform to the environmental regulations
of the country of origin.

Hodder & Stoughton Ltd
A division of Hodder Headline
338 Euston Road
London NW1 3BH

To our moms, Dorothy Lundin and Marilyn Dean,
who both died while we were writing this book and without
whom there would be no book at all

STEVE'S INTRODUCTION

When I first met Carr Hagerman I was immediately impressed and intrigued. He was a street performer and a self-taught student of business with little formal education, and he gave no quarter to matters of theory or reason. Our differences were enormous—I have a Ph.D. from a great academic institution and he was street smart—but what we shared was even larger. He saw in my work the expression of many of the values he had discovered as crucial to success in his work. I saw in him a new way to look at much of what I had come to take for granted.

Carr taught me, by example, how to speak, interact, engage, and just be in the world in a way that was consistent with my values, and I found his ideas provocative. He brought me on a journey to a new place in my work; a vibrant place with infinite possibilities, where things are simply accepted for what they are.

As we co-facilitated sessions and developed materials together, we also developed a bond that became stronger with each meeting. As my book *FISH!* became more and more successful, the demand for presentations became so great that we could no longer afford the luxury of working together. It was actually good timing because we had started stepping on each other's toes. So we went our separate ways, occasionally checking in from our respective hotels as we traveled the globe conducting *FISH!*-related programs.

And now, with delight, we once again merge our separate journeys as we bring to the written page our observations about the single biggest untapped force for good in any enterprise: We have come to call it *natural energy*. And our book focuses on how you can use this force in all your sales efforts in business and in life with dramatic results.

Organizations run best on natural energy and nowhere is this more true than in sales. When sales runs on natural energy, there are few toxic emissions, as natural energy burns clean with a mixture of spontaneous expression and commitment. It may sound impossible, but all that is often required to find a source of natural energy is a ten-degree turn of your head. Come along with us and you will see what we mean while meeting some rather unusual teachers.

PART ONE
BURNED OUT AND NEEDING A BOOST

Jim

My name is Jim and I sell for a living. Actually my name is Bartholomew James, but I prefer Jim. When you get right down to it, I think we all sell for a living. In a sense we all sell ourselves if nothing else.

I'm not a complicated guy. I took a good upbringing, complete with having to do regular chores; the traits I developed as an athlete; and my competitive spirit, and found a place in sales. While I have a business degree, it was my minor in science that guided me in choosing the industry in which I work.

I sell pharmaceutical products, some of which find their way to oncology patients who are provided a measure of hope that was not possible just a few years ago. I find that satisfying, although I sometimes get caught up in the selling process itself and forget some of the great things we do for people. The pharmaceutical industry has been portrayed somewhat negatively in the news lately, and it can be easy to forget the important role we play in sustaining a healthy society, but seeing the positive results on a daily basis helps.

And I think you sell, as well. I already said that, but it bears repeating. You might be selling a brand, a vision, an education, a direction, a service, the credibility of a set of numbers, learning to a student, or cereal to an infant, but I think we all sell for a living. Just my opinion, but that's what I believe.

I have done well in sales. In other words, I make good money. I have had the discipline to make more calls, send more letters, sponsor more events, and give more presentations than most of my colleagues. I have put in long days and worked on weekends. I almost never take vacation time, and I am proud of that fact. That has been my life. The founder of Radisson Inc. once said, "I keep up with the competition during the week and use the weekend to move ahead." I have tried to emulate that philosophy.

But recently I arrived at a place in my life where the discipline and willpower upon which I have built my success aren't enough. Longer hours don't seem to help at work. And in my life, what life I have, things are going in the wrong direction. I feel like I have reached a plateau at work and fallen behind in life. And to tell you the truth, I'm scared.

Today I'm starting a journey in search of a new source of energy. The problem is, I don't really know where to start. Perhaps something will show up if I pay attention. If something doesn't show up, I'm toast.

We typically use discipline and willpower when we start a diet, begin a self-improvement program, or want to sell more stuff and make a lot of money. Discipline and willpower almost always deliver, for a while.

A few monks can maintain a life based solely on discipline, but for most humans the price of a life ruled by discipline and willpower is simply too great over the long haul. There is just not enough juice to keep you going. Witness the dismal failure of more than 95 percent of those who attempt to lose weight by disciplined dieting. Eventually, another source of energy must be found.

To all who want a life that is both full of accomplishments and deeply satisfying, that source of energy becomes visible with only a ten-degree turn of your head. But when we are committed to a strategy, a ten-degree turn of the head is a waste of time.

Jensen Pharmaceuticals

Perhaps I should start by giving you a little background. I came to Jensen Pharmaceuticals right out of college. That's the way Jensen likes to hire new salespeople, green and flexible. I brought with me the discipline of a serious jock, a campus leader, and an "A" science student. I brought big goals and a competitive spirit. They told me I was a good match for Jensen Pharmaceuticals, and I was indeed.

My first year was frustrating because I had so much to learn, but challenging because I went right to work selling Jensen's products. In the beginning my district sales manager (DSM) would accompany me on my calls. Mia was a great DSM, and she knew just how to be supportive of my small gains while helping me learn better ways to work with clients.

Through formal corporate training programs and home study I learned about our products, the sales process, and how to fill out the numerous required forms. After four years in college, more schooling was not my first choice, but I knew I was lucky to be participating in one of the best training programs in the industry, so I sucked it up and learned everything I could that might help me be successful. And I loved being accountable for results from the very first day.

The second year was a blur of activity and I was assigned a mentor to help me continue my growth. My mentor was a seasoned rep who continued to work a territory. She was called a "master" by the company and seemed to really enjoy helping young sales representatives get established. She was my mom's age and knew the pharmaceutical business backward and forward. I learned a great deal about how to position our product and ways to gain access to decision makers.

At the end of the second year all of us "mentees" were brought together for a graduation ceremony. I knew most of them well by then as we took classes together, and I knew they were going to be hard to beat because they were a sharp bunch and from the best schools. Yeah, I'm competitive. That's why I chose sales.

My third year was a blast. I was finally getting used to the pressure of "stretch goals" for my territory, and I worked hard. My personal strategy for success was to play it by the numbers. More calls made, more presentations given, more events conducted and, as a result, more sales made. At the end of the year I was in the top 25 percent of the company and I was second among the members of my class. The woman who beat me lucked on to the Long Island territory but I wasn't going to let that be an excuse. Yeah, I'm competitive.

In the fourth year I asked Mia to work with me on my goals for the year and we met from time to time to check my progress. This process kept me both pumped and focused. The goal I chose with her encouragement was to become a Golden Eagle, a member of the top 5 percent club. I also wanted to beat the Long Island district salesperson and be number one in my class of trainees. I accomplished all three goals that year.

By the time my seventh year with Jensen rolled around, I had been awarded three Golden Eagles from success in two different territories. They sat proudly on my desk. I had purchased a townhouse in San Ramon; a hot sports car sat in the garage; and, for almost a year, I had been dating an enchanting redhead named Rebecca. My friends looked at me with envy, and life was really good! Well, pretty good anyway. OK, it might not have been so good. Actually, it sort of sucked.

I was having increasing difficulty finding the energy to maintain my high goals. This malady is common enough to have a name. It's called the "seventh-year slump." Let me share one of my journal entries so you can understand what I mean.

The Grind
(A Journal Entry)

I now know why you hear people call their work a grind.
We're all like coffee beans, whole and complete, then we get
tossed into the grinder so that we can release what's inside of
us. When all the beans are ground, what's left of us? Today I
am writing about my particular grind. I have poured my
life's energy into succeeding at work with little time for
anything else. And I haven't gotten around to roasting any
new beans.

Our team met recently to discuss an important but
difficult client. What made the meeting remarkable was the
fact that it involved one of my clients. I knew there was a
growing problem with this client, but no matter how much
time I spent or how many calls I made or how hard I worked,
I couldn't make any progress. The client had an endless
supply of issues and my usual song and dance was getting me
nowhere. Now the whole team was involved. I tend to be a
loner and I think some of the team members were enjoying
my discomfort.

The team was trying to be creative and all I had to offer

was persistence, or to "try harder." My boss actually stopped me at one point and suggested I listen to what was being said. It was not a great moment for me at work and I'm still not sure where to go with this client. It's an important piece of business.

Outside of work I was spending a great deal of time wondering how I might have more of a full life or have more access to things inside of me that might give my life a deeper sense of purpose. My girlfriend, Rebecca, has her own career as a customer service consultant and she does well. She is a couple years older than me and a lot wiser when it comes to leading a balanced life. Rebecca knows that right now we could not have a real life together given my work habits.

Rebecca says she admires my willpower but doesn't want to live, on a permanent basis, with someone who is so driven. I like Rebecca a lot and I'm feeling a huge amount of tension regarding my style of life. The fact that I flip back and forth between wanting more time with Rebecca and wanting more success at work is confusing to both of us.

A part of me has always loved children and would like a family someday. Rebecca and I seem to share many values and family is one of those. But we have decided to avoid subjects like that for a while, as we both recognize that I don't know how to make enough room in my life for any more than what we have.

Each day when I get up for work it is harder and harder to find the energy to carry on and I'm frightened that I will fall behind the competition. I put on a good face at work but

I'm concerned about my future and worried I will lose Rebecca.

There you have it. I don't know how to cut back. I like being a winner, a Golden Eagle. On the other hand, I miss spending time with friends and haven't had a real vacation since I started at Jensen. Well, like I said. It is confusing.

Every year Jensen ends up paying me for my unused vacation time as we are only allowed to carry over two weeks into a new year. My boss, Barbara, recently suggested I take some of that time for an actual vacation. She even implied that I might actually need it.

Mom

As is often the case in life, something unexpected can shake up a person's life and at the same time reveal a hidden path to the future. What I am about to relate is as clear as if it happened yesterday. It is here that this story really begins.

I was in the middle of our quarterly sales meeting when Jill, my assistant, slipped me a note. The little pink message said that my brother Perry was on the phone and holding. URGENT was written in Jill's neat block letters. My brother's name was underlined.

I admit my first impulse was irritation. We only had these meetings four times a year and, as a top salesperson, I enjoyed the attention and was expected to make a contribution to the team by giving them tips that would help them be more successful.

I thought about asking Jill to take a message. My brother Perry was prone to being dramatic. But Perry never called me at work. I excused myself quietly and received a slightly perturbed look from the SVP of

Sales, who was in the middle of her well-rehearsed presentation.

Jill was waiting just outside the conference room door. "Your brother seemed upset. I told him you were in a meeting and that you would call him back, but he said it was a family emergency."

"Thanks, Jill." I felt a stab of anxiety. The generally happy and energetic Jill looked concerned.

I walked back to my office and picked up the phone. "Perry, I'm right in the middle of an important sales meeting. What's up?"

"Mom is in the hospital; you need to get over here. It isn't good, Jim, not good at all."

"In the hospital? She was fine this weekend. What's wrong?" My brain began to fire random images of my mother's condition. A lifetime of heavy smoking did a number on her lungs and she would occasionally have trouble breathing. But in the hospital?

"Her lungs have failed, Jim. They got her all hooked up to tubes and wires . . . she fell . . . and the ambulance . . . there . . ."

In the few seconds that it took Perry to describe Mother's fall, a part of my mind drifted. Mom was in trouble? Impossible! Mom was a survivor, the rock in my world. She'll be OK. It was just Sunday when she'd called me to ask if I had read an article in the *Times* about traveling overseas and the great deals on airfares to England. That was two nights ago and everything was so normal, so ordinary.

"When will you get here?" Perry asked.

"I'm leaving right now."

"Have someone drive you, Jim. And get here as fast as is safe. The nurse is motioning for me so I'm going to hang up."

Fifteen minutes later Jill dropped me off at the hospital. Perry was outside Mom's door, his eyes swollen and red. He hugged me and took me inside. Mom was unconscious and breathing with the help of an oxygen mask. Each breath seemed labored.

As Perry and I sat at her bedside looking at the tentacles of modern medicine that were keeping her alive, I tried to find comfort, any comfort or hope that the situation would suddenly change and Mother would come around and regain her strength. When nurses came in to tend to her, I smiled and acted as if I'd done this a hundred times before. I tried to remain composed, confident, and casual, but it was bull; underneath my shiny exterior I was wracked with anxiety and a growing sadness the likes of which I'd never experienced. There was no strategy I could employ to get around what was happening. All I could do was to sit quietly and hold her frail hand.

Occasionally Perry and I would chat about something mundane: food, sports, politics.

At one point, I got up to look outside. It was a beautiful fall day and the sunlight made everything flush and full. The hospital window in our room was cracked open and the earthy smell of grass, trees, and flowers poured through the small gap and challenged the antiseptic sterility of the room. It was a confusing juxtaposition: on one side of the glass, the dark passing of my mother, straining to breathe, skin brittle and bruised; outside the glass, the unrestrained exuberance of bird and bug, trees dancing with the October breeze, and the safe rhythmic certainty of daylight.

A bee flew into the room, slipping through the opening and taking to flight once inside. It bounced off the ceilings and walked along the walls. It offered no threat but was instead something that felt like hope. Its chemical brain was driving it to search for sustenance, for some bounty it could carry on its hairy legs back to the hive. As I watched it search for signs and signals it could understand, the buzz of the bee became the only sound in the room. Mom was gone.

Then the gentle sobs of grieving brothers joined the small, erratic sounds of the small, insignificant insect buzzing and bouncing off the walls and ceiling. As my grief came upon me in full measure, I watched as the bee found its freedom again by following the beacon of the warm stream of sunlight and breeze flowing from outside. It was gone.

Nothing would ever be the same.

Mom's Legacy

The church was full to overflowing as my mom's friends, members of her parish, and others assembled to pay homage to her life. As I looked around the church I could see many in attendance who remembered her life in the theater.

Theater. I thought about her love of England and how she became so animated when we talked about the Globe Theatre and her favorite pubs. I had made a couple of business trips to London; after each, we would talk for hours. You would think she had spent a large portion of her life in England, but if she had it was mostly in her imagination, for her actual visits could be counted with the fingers on one hand. But what passion she had for the place.

Work looked different two days later. It had been a week since Mom died and there were many expressions of sympathy and the occasional well-intentioned but painful "she is in a better place" to greet me. And there was this haze. I don't know how to explain it but it felt like everything was in this haze.

When I met Rebecca for dinner I tried to explain it to her, but instead started bawling like a baby. That night I could swear I heard a bee buzzing around the townhouse. Ordinarily I would worry about getting stung in my sleep but it was strangely comforting and I was out like a light.

I handled grief like many men; I immersed myself in work. This should have been easy for a workaholic like me. But when I called on the discipline I considered my secret weapon, something felt different. Willpower didn't seem to be enough anymore.

While my sales results were steady, I knew the reason was past effort, not present activity. I was losing ground and it would be visible to all in less than a year. I had no idea what to do.

There were times when I would be sitting in a hotel room and looking at the bland room service food when a thought popped into my head and I realized I would have given a king's ransom to talk, really talk, about what I was feeling.

Busy soon wore thin and I started to feel like I had to do something, anything, that would lead me to recapture a sense of aliveness. Somehow, I thought, if I just kept moving, my sadness wouldn't find me, it wouldn't track me down as I hid in the shadows of my work. I was wrong.

I returned from a road trip to the outer reaches of my territory and was taking my suitcase out of the trunk when I saw the large cardboard file box I had put there the day we distributed Mom's possessions. Later I opened the box. It contained the last of my mother's personal effects that I had to go through, and it was the one box my mother had kept close to her.

"Jim," she had said on one of my visits. "This box has all the most important paperwork in it." There were pages of paper that my mother had labeled IMPORTANT LIFE AND DEATH PAPERWORK. Mom was incredibly practical. "After I bite the dust you'll find all the important stuff in here." It was a small, somewhat tattered cardboard file box full of various and sundry items, paperwork, scrapbooks, and high school yearbooks. There were a few letters she'd saved from her brothers. There were old black-and-white pictures of her and them standing on the shore of Grand Lake, Colorado, each smiling in their youth. At the bottom of the pile was an envelope of old pictures from her many trips, and a travel brochure for London.

Near the bottom of the box was another high school yearbook, this one from West High School, class of 1942. The book was full of black-and-white photos of clean-cut, earnest, and hopeful-looking young people. The margins of many pages were full of handwritten missives of luck and good cheer from long-forgotten friends of my mother. A number of the names were familiar. I realized they had come to her funeral all these years later.

The Camera

I felt a surge of emotion as I uncovered an unexpected surprise at the bottom of the box, a small 35mm camera. Though I'd dug through the box before, I'd somehow missed the camera.

I blew off some of the dust that had gathered on the rough black exterior of the camera. I remembered giving this very camera to my mother as a Christmas present sometime in the late 1970s. It became her constant companion. It was a fixture at holiday gatherings and family get-togethers at Grand Lake in the summer. She took pictures of her dog and her cats and the places she visited. She also took many pictures of England.

Mom wasn't much of a photographer. She would groan with disappointment as she sifted through her developed pictures, "Damn, another headless person . . . I think that's you . . . I think."

I noticed that there were undeveloped pictures still

imprisoned in the camera, half a roll of used pictures waiting to have their stories released. I wondered what they'd be of, perhaps pictures of family gatherings.

A few weeks after I'd found the camera, I took the half-used roll of film in for processing. When I got it back, I was surprised that there were no pictures of people. There were twelve beautiful pictures of her garden in perfect summer bloom. The story she left behind was one of cultivating life, of liberating beauty from a seed, and her tolerance of garden anarchy.

I wasn't disappointed; it was the perfect footnote to her last months of life. It made me happy, and it made me sad. I suddenly felt grim and alone.

Inside the envelope of photographs was a coupon for use when purchasing more film, along with details about some travel photo contest. The coupon featured a layout of what looked to be vacation photos from London and it featured happy families smiling and enjoying life. It said CAPTURE YOUR LIFE across the top. Below that was printed:

THE WORLD IS OUT THERE IN FULL COLOR.
CAPTURE IT AND BRING IT HOME.

I grabbed a pen and immediately wrote:

- Talk to Mia
- Call Brenda at the Travel Desk and book a vacation trip to London

- Stop the newspaper
- Ask Rebecca if she can go with me
- Buy film
- Take a deep breath
- Try not to feel guilty about taking a vacation

PART TWO
FINDING MYSELF

The Hat

It was late afternoon in London and following a short nap, I decided to walk the streets of central London in search of something to eat. Restaurants and pubs are everywhere in this part of the city. There weren't the big-scale chain restaurants like I'd find at home, though McDonald's, Pizza Hut, and Burger King have British offspring. No, the eateries there seemed to grow like weeds out of every crack in the wall. Sandwich boards touting ORIGINAL FISH & CHIPS! and other tourist cuisine were visible on nearly every street. Pub signs with names like the Cock and Crow, or the Strafford Ale House, hung over cracked sidewalks and crowded the view down most any street.

I had asked Rebecca to join me on the trip, but she was in the middle of a major work engagement. "I think you need to do this alone, Jim," she had said. Like I said, she is a wise woman.

My boss was extremely supportive as she should have been, given that it was her idea. "You've been pushing real hard for a number of years. If you didn't take some time now I might have had to insist."

I wandered out the door of the hotel and down a small side street that emerged at Oxford Street. I passed a small pub buzzing with afternoon activity. Glancing in, I could see what appeared to be local office workers holding glasses of ale and occasionally a cigarette. Men with loosened ties gathered in clusters, drinking their pints and laughing at the day's most absurd events.

As I continued along Oxford Street, I felt like a fish swimming upstream. People bounced off me like bumper cars with hardly a comment. Out in the street the late-afternoon rush hour was overwhelming. Cabs traveled back and forth like field mice, darting among the red double-decker elephants occasionally.

It was so noisy and crowded that in the midst of this mayhem I could not have felt more alone. After walking a couple of blocks, I looked up to see that I was standing in front of a Selfridges department store. Mom used to talk about this store and how she loved to shop here when she was in London. I wasn't feeling much like shopping, but I felt compelled to wander through the big doors and see what the store was all about. Perhaps I could lift the feeling of intense loneliness.

Thinking that walking through Selfridges would be a respite from the late-afternoon commotion, I soon came to realize, was incorrect. The store had a rush hour of its own going. The aisles were crammed with shoppers carrying bags of merchandise. Two large escalators located in the middle of the main floor added to the visual confusion, with a queue of people waiting to catch a ride up to clothing and notions, while other people seemed to disappear as the escalator escorted them to furniture and foods.

A live band played between the escalators, adding to the din. I stood dumbfounded. Sure, I'd been in department stores before, but none of them was ever this busy, this packed, or this vital. I stood off to one side so as not to block the flow of consumers. Mostly these people were well-dressed professionals or upscale city dwellers. There were also a notable number of tourists, identifiable by the cameras that hung around their necks or the large canvas bags that hung over their shoulders.

As the crowd flowed by me, I noticed a tall, distinguished-looking man wearing a top hat and tails and sporting an ornate walking cane. He seemed to command a large space of his own. A smile as regal as his fine clothing adorned his face. He occasionally nodded his head and pinched the corner of his hat with his left hand as he worked through the sea of people. His voice had a Caribbean lilt.

Frequently someone would stop to greet him or to get pictures taken with him. When one group of middle-aged women with thick German accents stopped to take his picture, he said, "Of course, my ladies, but please, allow me to prepare." He then produced a set of white gloves out of his pocket and pulled them over his long fingers. The women gathered around him and he stood with his chin held high, never stooping to do anything so plebian as putting his arms around them. His smile elevated the room.

A few customers greeted him by name, calling it out as they walked by. He greeted children with ample kindness and never seemed to be surprised by anyone or anything. He acted as if these were all his friends.

I later learned a great deal more about this tall, elegant man, but I was intrigued from the moment I first saw him. The dreadlocks spilling in all directions from under the formal hat were enough of a juxtaposition to catch anyone's eye.

I thought that surely he was a hired hand, a performer of some sort that Selfridges had brought in to entertain the shoppers. When he walked by me and smartly greeted me with "sir," he also gently saluted and winked. I stood transfixed and watched him continue through the flow of people, finally disappearing around a corner.

"Isn't he great!" I looked over to see a tall woman with beautiful brown wavy hair, emerald green eyes, and a smile full of bright and perfect teeth. "He walks through here a couple times a week."

"He's not hired to do this?"

"No. He lives nearby and just likes to dress up and make people feel good." She said this as she rearranged perfume bottles on her countertop. "He told me his grandmother had left him a spot of money when she died and that he didn't need to work anymore. He told my friend that he had good luck in the stock market. And I read a brief article about him once that said he was once a top sales agent for a firm that sold computer software. Who knows? But what he does now is make people smile."

"Is it some kind of character he's playing or is he just dressing up to be . . . interesting?" I asked.

She laughed. "If you ask Top Hat about what's up with the top hat and the tails and the walking stick and all that, he'll say, 'My lady, I'm no actor and this is no costume; I'm a gentleman, and this is what gentlemen wear,'" she said, laughing and slapping her countertop. "He's a gentleman and people love it. When he stops a group of people will gather to talk with him, get his picture, and ask for directions to the loo. Wonderful really. He just seems to generate so much interest and energy, wherever he goes. "

"Did you say his name was Top Hat?" I asked.

"Yes, sir. No one knows his real name; we all just call him Top Hat. When he first started coming here, security would follow him around because they thought he might be, you know, a little off. But now, they like it when he's here; it's like he belongs here. That's the Hat."

"Thanks. That's different."

"No. That's Top Hat."

"Of course it is," I responded with a grin. "What else would you call a gentleman?"

"Cheers!" she said as I walked away.

What a curious thing for someone to do, to walk around dressed like that and draw attention. I continued walking around the store, but began to feel more than a little claustrophobic, and decided to leave.

I thought about that top hat man and how much fun

he must have. I even felt a bit of jealousy. It had been a while since I had that kind of free-flowing fun. And he just seemed natural at it. His energy attracted those around him like a human magnet. Top Hat was simply being Top Hat and he spoke to me in ways I did not fully understand.

Oddly, the fact that I was thinking about this Top Hat person made me uneasy at first. Why would I care about some guy walking around with a silly top hat on? But the more I thought my thinking was silly, the more curious I became. I was intrigued.

How can someone like me, in a regular job, find that kind of energy for my work?

Trafalgar Square

Over the next couple of days I devoted a lot of time to writing in my journal and drinking expensive coffee drinks at Pret a Manger, my favorite spot from which to observe people. I sat by the window to get the best light and the best view of the Londoners weaving their way along the busy sidewalk that bordered Trafalgar Square.

At the moment my attention was drawn to the fountain in the square. That's how I noticed an old man with a burlap bag on his shoulder. His face was carved with deep lines, and graying sprays of eyebrows protruded from his forehead. His ears were thick and wide under his plaid hat.

He seemed on a mission as he strolled near the fountain with a keen concentration on the tourists. You knew they were tourists; they were taking pictures and chasing the pigeons. I had heard that London authorities have tried to rid the square of pigeons, using every technique the public would accept, but to no avail. Pigeons liked the square and the tourists seemed to like the pigeons.

Many people would stand with their arms out, empty-handed and silent, not moving, hoping the pigeons would find their arms, shoulders, or head an attractive place to land. But pigeons have their own agenda, their own daily to-do list, and there are only two things listed. One is to eat, and I'll leave the other to your imagination.

The old man with the burlap sack would spot a tourist trying to attract pigeons and would wander over to them and, while furtively looking over his shoulder, would fill their hands with seeds and then quietly walk away. The pigeons would flock to these tourists who now were sporting pigeon gold: seeds! Soon the pigeons would cover these people, standing on shoulders, heads, arms, and circling above the people's heads. Other people nearby would watch and hold their arms out, but these hungry scavengers were only interested in the outstretched arms of the seed givers. The old man stood at a distance and smiled.

I made another entry in my journal.

The sight of a tourist in Trafalgar Square with empty hands and arms extended, waiting for a pigeon, reminds me that you always need to offer something if you want to attract anything. I have kept my arms outstretched at work until my shoulders ached and I would bite my lip and hold them out even longer. How long have I been out of seeds? What do I have to offer now?

The Globe Theatre

I decided to wander down to the river and visit the Globe stage. My mother had always wanted to visit this reproduction of Shakespeare's theater but never did. It was a perfect day, and the paths were full of people wandering along the bank of the river, stopping for pictures and unfolding maps to find coordinates. I wandered by the Tate Modern, its green lawn covered with people sitting on grass and benches, some playing Frisbee. I could see the roofline of the old Globe come into view. I soon found myself standing at the wrought-iron gates in front of the Globe.

I was overwhelmed. It seemed like everything I was learning, the challenges I'd had since Mom died and the intense moments of emotional anguish, somehow met here. I felt deeply sad but curiously awake and invigorated. I entered the facility and bought a ticket for the tour. Five minutes later I was wandering with strangers into the courtyard, and then into the confines of the theater itself.

The theater was an immense treasure to the eye. Built as an exact replica of Shakespeare's Globe, it was colorful and extraordinarily beautiful. There was a deep sense of place here, a connection to something old and profound. I stood oblivious to the tour guide's historical descriptions, choosing instead to remain in contact with my own silence and awe.

After the tour was over, we passed through a lobby before being escorted to a gift shop. In the lobby was a large wall full of beautiful brass plates, each the same size, each placed neatly next to the other. Each plate was engraved with a name or signature. As I stood in front of the shining brass wall, I decided to purchase a plate for my mother, to have her name gleaming in the wings of the Globe.

Mom always thought I had some kind of natural charisma with people. Then again, she was my mom. She encouraged me to find a way to make use of this charisma in creative ways. One time, on a trip to Seattle in my senior year of high school, we were wandering through the Museum of Modern Art when she stopped in front of a Picasso, pointed, and said, "If you look at your life sideways, you just might find some interesting expression of your own."

I caught a glimmer of what she was saying. I'd become good at my job, and at the same time had developed an emptiness inside. I wasn't living an authentic performance. I wasn't looking sideways at my life; I was just standing with my arms outstretched waiting for the real life to come along, to find me. I was just so comfortable. I sat and wrote:

There is an old saying that all life is a stage, but is that really true since that statement doesn't account for the wings, the offstage, and the unlit shadows behind the curtain? Perhaps it is better to say that we are all players in search of a stage or running from the stage, and that very few of us are actually onstage.

Covent Garden

With another promising day of exploration dangling in front of me, I headed out in the general direction of Covent Garden, having been told it contained an open-air market and entertainment. I was in no hurry, but was simply determined to eventually arrive there.

"It's where young people like you go," the hotel desk clerk had said. "Just be careful of those who might want to remove your wallet," he added with a smile.

Covent Garden turned out to be what all themed retail experiences aspire to be: busy with good shops and unique boutiques; full of colorful architecture; and constantly entertaining. It would seem to be popular, as well, since it was the middle of the afternoon on a Thursday and the place was packed.

I browsed through some of the shops, mostly looking at other people doing the same thing. One woman, apparently French, carried so much merchandise that she could barely walk, while an older woman who looked like she had a history with this place simply stood on the corner glaring at a passerby.

At one end of the market was an old church framed by big stone pillars. Cobblestone covered the area just outside the church. As I approached, I noticed a large crowd, perhaps sixty people, had gathered to watch a street performer who was standing atop a large, aluminum ladder. The church provided a convenient backdrop for the performance and served as a sound barrier.

As the show progressed, more and more people gathered, stayed, and became interested in the energy of the place. The performer seemed to grow in confidence and the audience got into a groove with him. It felt rhythmic, jazzlike. It was compelling. The show ended with enthusiastic applause and the audience began lining up to drop money into the performer's hat. The investment had paid off.

I'd seen performers work on the streets before and always loved it. My mother and I stopped to watch street performers often in our travels together, from Washington Square in New York to the Boulder Mall in Boulder, Colorado. We often wondered why more cities in America didn't have street performers. Later I read that most cities don't want street performers. Street performers often bend the rules and always work outside the lines. I remember sharing this with Mom. She shook her head and responded, "That's the point, isn't it? Sometimes what we can't control is the most interesting and attractive aspect of a situation."

I took a seat at a small outdoor café located just

adjacent to the church and cobblestones. Each table was small with a large, red umbrella sprouting through a small hole in its center. My table sat at the boundary of the sidewalk and the café, allowing me a view of shoppers, shops, and street performers alike.

Why am I here?

The sun and lazy summer breeze conspired with my mind, and my thoughts filled with images of work and home. I had everything going for me back home and yet I was sure something important was missing. Work had simply become too much like work.

Is that my destiny, lifeless work? And longer hours as the only option for maintaining the same or perhaps even lower results?

Top Hat Appears

"Excuse me, sir, are you all right?"

I recognized the Caribbean lilt, and looked up to see the dapper man with a cane and hat. It was Top Hat.

"I'm fine, sir. Just thinking about things, but thanks for your concern."

"And I'm sorry if I disturbed your thoughts. Are you here to watch the buskers?"

"Bus what? I don't know," I offered. "What the heck is a busker?"

The gentleman laughed, and pointed with his long black cane in the direction of the cobblestones and church.

"Oh, a street performer?" I said.

"Call it what you want, sir, but here we call them buskers. What, may I ask, brings you to London?"

"I was just thinking." I paused. How much did I want to tell this guy? "Actually, I came here because I needed a break from my job, wanted to have some rest and relaxation, you know, a vacation and that kind of thing."

"I see! A vacation is a good thing, my man. We call it 'going on holiday.' We all need to rest, to reinvigorate our imaginations. We all need to reconnect with ourselves."

He said all this with a consistent smile. His face was large and smooth and his eyes clear. He stood with such stability, as if wherever he was standing he had roots that anchored him to the ground. He moved slowly and deliberately. Long white gloves covered his hands, and that beautiful silk top hat perched comfortably on his head.

"May I partake of your company, good sir?" he asked with perfect diction.

"Sure. Please, sit down. My name's Jim."

He took off his hat and set it on the table, then pulled off each white glove, laying them on the hat.

"Let me buy you a drink," I offered.

"Brilliant. I'll have a glass of tap water, no olives, extra wet with a twist." The waiter came by and I repeated the order, which caused the waiter to laugh. Top Hat seemed to be content to sit and consider the view.

"I saw you over at Selfridges. You were posing for pictures and greeting people."

He looked off in the distance, his face calm and content. "I know, I saw you, as well." He looked at me. "I have a photographic memory for faces. Perhaps we all do."

His glass of water arrived, though it was sporting a cocktail umbrella. "How clever, an umbrella for a field mouse." He folded it up and put it to the side.

"The woman at Selfridges said that you dress up like

this just for kicks, because it's fun, and that you go by the name of Top Hat."

"You are misinformed, sir, though not entirely. I'm indeed Top Hat; my friends and acquaintances call me 'the Hat'; but I don't do this just for kicks. I am an ambassador of goodwill. I live for civility and courteous discourse, elements I believe our modern society is letting slip away."

"Are you a performer or a busker like those guys?" I asked.

"No, sir. I'm no longer a street performer, not really, although I gave it a fling. It is correct to say that I'm a gentleman!" He said this with dignity.

"I can see that, but to do what you're doing, I mean, why do you dress up like this and walk around the streets of London and entertain people?"

He shifted in his seat and turned his face and sizeable frame toward me. "I don't see this as dressing up. I see my job in the world as messenger, and my message is about grace and the importance of kindness." He sat back in his chair.

"Why the outfit?"

"It's a simple thing. The clothes create the man. What you wear helps define who you are. But it doesn't stop at the thread; it goes down into the blood. It is dress like this that starts to tell the rest of the world my story. It creates a natural connection and relationship with others. It's creative and lively, it's curious and strange, and those are things people find most attractive." He smiled again: "We all have something that helps define us, you know, like a business suit or attaché case, maybe the white coat if you're working in a doctor's office. It is just my way of getting myself worked up, feeling complete. What kind of work do you do back home?"

"Actually, I sell drugs. Wait a minute; let me clarify that. I sell legitimate pharmaceutical products in the U.S." Then I blurted out, "My mother passed away recently and she loved it here. So I decided to visit the place she loved and just perhaps find something of my own."

"I see. So you came here, all the way across the pond, to find solace?" he said with a soft lilt in his voice.

"I guess so," I answered. "My mother and I were close. Dad bailed when I was young. So we were a pair. She was/is directly connected to my heart and it's been . . . well . . ." I stopped as I felt my throat constrict.

We sat in silence as the din of the place spilled over us. There was comfort in the commotion.

"My mother is deceased, as well, my friend. It was the hardest day of my life. I have my version of your feelings. These are feelings those of us lucky to live long enough will all feel one day."

He stared at the sky for the moment, and he smiled again and looked at me. "But what you describe, the connection with your mother, that is something that doesn't disappear, it is the energy of life working its magic.

"We have to be open to the magic of life," he continued. "That is why I'm the Hat, because one day I was going through the closet in my mother's room and I found this beautiful silk hat in a box that said 'James Locke Hat Company, St James Place, London.' I pulled out this lovely top hat and put it on my head. It fit! It fit like it was made for me. I was intrigued by the hat and felt energy wearing it. I decided then to try some other clothing, the tuxedo, the tails, and gloves. I stood in front of the mirror and," he laughed, "I thought I looked like an idiot!" He laughed again with the steady breath of a kind man, a laugh grounded in the heart.

Top Hat leaned across the table and in a lower voice he said, "I also felt a shock of energy, I felt taller, handsome, certain of myself. I thought, *This is what Superman might have felt when he changed into his clothes with the big S on the front.* I looked into that mirror, with my hat on, and I tipped it forward and said, 'Afternoon ma'am,' and I felt alive.

"I originally came here to perform magic tricks and be a comedian, but it didn't work for me. I wasn't wired to be that kind of busker. Magic tricks and all that just seemed like a distraction. I'm not an actor or entertainer! I did discover that people seemed attracted to me, wanted to be around me. They complimented me, told me how much they enjoyed my kind demeanor, and wanted pictures. Before I knew it, I was walking around London greeting people. I noticed that people were energized when they were around the Hat. Eventually I chose to be my own 'ambassador of goodness.'"

He took a sip of water. He held his glass with studied elegance. He pulled out a handkerchief and dabbed his forehead.

"So what do you get out of this?" I asked.

"I do it for the energy of it." He sat back again and

linked his fingers together and rested his hands across his chest. A burst of laughter could be heard not too far away. "What I really want is to have others recognize something special in themselves when they see what I uncovered in myself. When we can see each other as unique, it makes each of us feel special.

"What most people do not recognize is that these street performers aren't really any different from a man who works for a big drug company. You see, so many people watch the buskers and they are thinking to themselves, *I wish I could do that. I wish I could make people laugh, or juggle fire torches.* Mostly what they mean is, *I wish I had the courage.*"

"Courage, to be in front of people?" I asked.

"No, not really. The courage to access the freedom we all have to create something out of nothing and not get lost in how it's going to work out. The courage to have a bit more trust in ourselves."

A bee landed on the table and, in a search for something sweet, it located the top of the open bottle of soda.

"Buskers bring life to the corners, alleys, and paths. They carry on the happy tradition of the juggler, the jester, and the fool. When you let yourself be free to actually be yourself, regardless of what others think, you're on the same track."

"I don't know if I get that. I mean, these performers all need applause, the audience version of appreciation, so isn't that kind of against what you are saying? Be yourself, as long as there is applause?" I asked.

"No! The best buskers use the applause as a way to

build more energy, but they aren't driven by it alone. The good ones have something to say, something they want the world to see, something they are inspired by, and they are driven to share it, to show it off, to build something out of what is burning in their guts."

He took another sip of his fancy tap water and gently flicked the energetic bee away. "You see, buskers are working with an energy source that is available to any of us. The best of them understand that engagement with the audience produces natural energy. This natural energy is the most powerful energy on the planet. It has changed human history, built great things, provoked great artistic impressions, musical works, and virtually all the companies in the world. It is the energy that caused you to get up and try again until you could take that first step as a child.

"Many never stop to think that the large office buildings in every major city in the world were the result of an idea in the mind of an entrepreneur. They did not fall from the sky as fully formed corporations complete with headquarters. They started as an idea fueled by natural energy. Natural, human, energy divided and multiplied is a force that is nearly unstoppable."

His eyebrows rose into his forehead. "What a busker does is create a focal point for the energy, like a magnifying glass does for the hot summer sun. Once you tap that energy, you can do almost anything. What's more, as a performer, or as Top Hat in my case, this energy keeps things fresh, never boring. The secret is in letting go of"—he leaned across the table—"control."

I thought about my most-alive and successful work relationships. When I was working with my favorite colleagues and we were fully engaged, I could feel the flow of energy between us and it seemed unstoppable, almost fierce. And no one was in control.

"I think I understand that," I said, "but it's easy to do when you are making people happy wearing a tux, or juggling a chain saw, or doing a handstand over a bucket of burning coal. Where I work, it's all about the tie and shiny shoes, reports and graphs, data sets and projections, goals and objectives, and blah blah blah. It sucks the energy out of you and leaves you exhausted."

"I would guess that is because you're doing it alone." He said this as he looked at some shoppers passing by.

"No, I work as a part of a sales group and there are thirty-five hundred employees in our headquarters building. I'm definitely not alone!" I corrected him.

"Please don't take offense, but if you are working with your own energy and not tapping into the deeper well of the energy in those around you, then you are working alone. Yes, there are many others nearby, but they are just backdrops in your life scene. Are you a one-man band, Jim? Isn't it true you work alone?"

I was stunned. I took a deep breath and responded. "Yes," I heard a small, distant voice respond. "Yes, I work alone."

"As you seem to have discovered, Jim, a one-person band eventually reaches a natural limit. No wonder you're exhausted."

The natural rhythms of the world are all around us and bristling with energy. This energy is available to fuel what we do in life. To start the flow of natural energy, all that is necessary is to fully engage another human being. Working alone is a choice, not a requirement.

The Envelope

Top Hat pulled a letter-size, sealed envelope from inside his suit jacket. The tattered envelope was a startling contrast to his spotless suit and hat. You could see where it had been folded many times and it was smudged and creased.

"This envelope represents an old tradition among a special group of buskers. A young talent in search of his or her place in the world of street performers sees a seasoned busker perform and wants to know everything the pro knows, for the cost of a cup of coffee. Now there is nothing wrong with that—most of us are happy to help a newcomer—but we need a way to separate the curious from the committed. The envelope does that."

He pushed it across the table with a warm smile.

"If you decide to develop your skills of engagement, this envelope will be helpful. It is your introduction to the next part of your journey and the source of natural energy. When and if you decide to take the next step, take this envelope to Dublin and find the Rat Catcher.

Just remember, the seal cannot be broken. The envelope must be intact if you want to learn what the Rat Catcher has to teach you."

"That's in Ireland? A rat catcher in Ireland?"

"Right. When you get to Dublin, look for Grafton Street. It's easy to find. Then walk from the top to the bottom of the street, a good many blocks for sure. While you're walking, look for a large crowd gathered around a busker. The busker you are looking for is balding, wears old rags, and is prone to hyperbole. Don't worry; you'll know it's him when you find him. Look for a busker standing in the center of a circle outlined by a red rope."

I took all this in and made a few notes and then muttered under my breath, "Red rope, rat catcher, right."

"He is called the Rat Catcher. His name dates back to the time of the plague in Europe when a courageous group of men went house to house selling their skills in catching the rats that spread the plague."

"And if I find him and his red rope, what then?"

"You sound a bit skeptical, Jim."

"Well, you know, it does sound a bit unusual."

"And a top hat is not?"

"Good point."

"Give the Rat Catcher this envelope and offer to buy him a cup of coffee. He will first check the envelope to see that it hasn't been opened. If he accepts the envelope, it means he will work with you, but only if you show him you are committed to becoming a top performer in your field."

"Top performer?"

"Isn't that what you want to be?"

"Yes. Most definitely! And this rat guy has something to tell me about being a top performer?"

"That he does. The Rat Catcher can tell you some amazing things about performance. I bet he knows things I don't even know I don't know. In my opinion, the Rat Catcher is a great next step in your journey.

"Here is something to consider. If the Rat Catcher and other street performers didn't understand energy, they wouldn't eat. In order to be a top performer as a busker, you must know a lot about energy; especially the natural energy, for which buskers have invented their own language.

"I want you to visit the Rat Catcher because he is so good at what he does that other buskers come to him for advice and counsel. He can teach you how to become a top performer by teaching you the language of energy. Then it is up to you to claim what you have learned."

"Like the energy that flows when you replace working alone with human engagement. There is a language for that?"

"Exactly. And when you have learned all that the Rat Catcher has time to teach you, come back and look me up so we can finish our conversation."

With that, Top Hat patted the top of the envelope, looked me in the eye, tipped his hat, and excused himself, quickly disappearing into the crowd. I found myself stammering an additional quick thank-you to the back of a quickly disappearing hat.

You've Got to Be Kidding!!

I sat for a long time thinking about my discussion with Top Hat. And then I was overcome with an intense episode of common sense. It was enticing to think there might be a "Rat Catcher" with a "language of energy" waiting in Dublin for me. Common sense, however, suggested I was being conned.

I decided right then that I wouldn't extend my stay or travel to Dublin to look for the Rat Catcher. I'd come to my senses, thankfully, and I didn't need to follow some Top Hat treasure hunt to buried riches. I had a life at home; so what if I was a bit bored at work? The insight about not going it alone was powerful and would surely give me the boost I needed. And if it didn't, I would just have to suck it up and do it with hard work.

With the fat part of the day remaining before my scheduled flight, I decided to see more of the city and I wandered around, visiting museums and pointedly staying away from buskers. Yet I saw them everywhere. I took the Queens Walk, under the London Eye Ferris wheel, and there were buskers. I walked through Piccadilly Circus, and there were drummers and scammers, a juggler, and a man playing the pipes. Each time I came upon a busker, I found myself wanting to stop and enjoy it, to see what he—or occasionally she—had to offer. But I did what I do best. I controlled the impulse and passed the time in other ways.

As I waited for my checked luggage and then a cab to the train station, I felt resolved to get back to my work and quit my whining. I had a job that paid well and had super benefits. Why was I so self-centered that I thought my life had to be perfect? If I just worked a bit harder during the day and if I was a bit smarter about getting energy from others on the team, I could get my job performance back where it needed to be—and find time to have more of a life. I simply needed to put what I had just learned to work.

But as the cab pulled away from the hotel I was feeling a bit sad, as well. This trip had been full of revelations and some personal closure. I was glad I came and was strangely hesitant to leave.

Notes from the Plane Ride Home

What an amazing trip. I had no real agenda in going to England, it just seemed like the right thing to do and it was. I'm returning to my job and my life in the U.S. with a gift from a Caribbean man who walks the streets simply being a gentleman.

I understand now that discipline and willpower account for much of my success, but for the long term, more natural forms of energy need to be found. Top Hat has helped me see that those I meet along my journey can be sources of energy and I don't need to go it alone.

I have seen others as distractions that absorb precious time and keep me from achieving my goals. I can't wait to try the new approach. Perhaps I will even find time for a life outside of work.

PART THREE
NOW WHAT?

Back on the Job

I arrived at work on a dead run and full of energy. A special meeting of the sales team had been arranged for my benefit and I was excited to start working on my plan to engage others on the team. We assembled in the conference room and as I took my chair, I realized the last memory I had of this room was the day my brother called from the hospital. I willed myself back to the present.

Mia opened the meeting. "I know we are all interested in what Jim has been doing. Jim, bring us up to speed."

I decided to share a bit of my adventure before I got into the specifics. I had just started when Robb reached for his pulsating phone. He looked down at the phone and quietly left, not to return. I had done that many times myself and didn't think too much about it. There were now seven of us around the table and within five minutes we were down to four. I cut off my remarks about Top Hat and got to the bottom line.

"I realized in a flash that I had pretty much become a solo player fueled entirely by hard work and discipline. It was becoming harder and harder to get motivated each day. Top Hat helped me understand that there is a continuous flow of energy in the world in the form of other people and I want to tap into that energy source. So if you see me wanting to get more connected with you in the future, don't be surprised."

Mark, always the politician, spoke first. "That's really nice, Jim. We know this has been a tough few weeks for you and you have our support, buddy. Stop by any time, man. It sounds like it was a cool trip and I want to hear more about it." And that was it.

The others nodded and Mia concluded the meeting by saying, "Welcome back, Jim. We're all pleased that you have found what you were looking for and we will help in any way we can." Those who remained left quickly, starting their phone conversations as they passed the threshold.

I was slow to pick up my things. The session was not exactly what I'd planned. Mia held back by the door and then came back and sat next to me.

"Want to talk to me about it, Jim?"

A passionate flow of words erupted from deep inside me. "I had this fantastic insight in London and I guess I expected to be able to just pass it along to everyone else and they would be excited as well! It didn't quite work out that way. I had a lapse in memory about how fast the motor runs here. In a couple days my motor will be running the same way. What did I expect? Did I really expect them to stop thinking about their clients and hang on my every word just because I had a moment of personal insight? But even though I realize all of that, I feel let down."

"Jim, we have a hard-working and diverse sales team but reflection and creativity have not been our strengths. When you started talking about the guy with the hat who is a gentleman, it may have been a bit much for our down-to-business team. Why don't you tell me what you learned in England? I would really like to understand."

"Mia, I was talking to this guy and telling him about how my energy was waning and how discipline and hard work didn't seem to be enough anymore. And he said maybe it's time to stop working alone. And I said I work with a team, and as I said it I realized I may belong to a team but I draw no energy from the team because I do work alone. Most of us work alone. And I got real excited about finding another way to work. A way that relies less on nose-to-grindstone and more on drawing energy from human interaction. It was like this flash, Mia. And I wanted to get back here as fast as possible and put it to work even though the Hat seemed to think I had more to learn."

"More to learn?"

And I decided to tell Mia about the envelope and the Rat Catcher and a few of the things I had glossed over. When I was finished Mia just smiled at me and there was a twinkle in her eye.

"What? Do you think I've been taken by a trickster?"

"Not at all. I think you met someone who provoked

your curiosity and got you thinking about the importance of energy. Almost every salesperson I have ever known eventually has an energy crisis like yours. We work so hard making the engine of commerce run but we often do it alone, and we believe the primary source of energy we can rely on is based on self-motivation, getting pumped up to face another day, and discipline. It is all self-centered.

"I can see why you're excited. You were able to catch a glimpse of another way to approach work and you want to share your excitement with the rest of us.

"But I think you do need to consider the suggestions of that Top Hat guy. You have the insight but you have none of the tools. Perhaps that's what still awaits you in Dublin."

"I feel a little silly. I come back with a story about a tall man who walks the streets of London in a costume and I expect the team to share my excitement without sharing the experience. Dumb. They must wonder if I'm losing it. Hey, thanks for helping me put it in perspective."

"That's what DSMs are for," she said, laughing. "And I meant what I said. See how the next couple of weeks work out and if you decide to continue the journey, you have lots of vacation left and I will personally cover your clients."

"Wow. That's really thoughtful. I know you have a full plate."

"Perhaps, but it is also selfish. This may be a boondoggle or it may be one of the best things that ever happened to our team. If it turns out to be real, I think we all could take a lesson or two from Top Hat and that other guy."

"The Rat Catcher."

"How could I forget." Mia laughed again.

The next two weeks were familiar because they could have been any two weeks of the last few years. Nothing really changed at all. Prospecting, cold calls, preparing proposals, follow-up, sponsoring events, new product orientations, paperwork, and occasional conversations with other agents continued to be the main activities in my life. But something had changed. The conversations I had with customers and other sales reps felt awkward and stilted. I wanted to have a more genuine connection but couldn't figure out exactly how to make it happen. My attempts fell flat and were ineffective at best, and at worst insincere.

I realized I typically treat my clients as sources of income with little time spent to engage them in a free-form style. But approaching in a free-form way might take a few extra moments and my success is built on volume. The many things I think of as things I am doing for my clients, like remembering birthdays and children's names, are really formula driven. My routine is primarily designed to serve me and to put money in my account with the least possible fuss. And for that I am considered a winner, a Golden Eagle. *But am I really alive?*

At that moment I knew I wanted to change. But wanting to change and knowing how to do it are two different things.

One part of my life had changed for the better. I was spending more time with Rebecca. And Rebecca had joined Mia in encouraging me to go to Dublin and finish what I started. I try to be a smart man, so I listened.

Looking for the Rat Catcher

And so I found myself in Dublin just weeks after saying good-bye to Top Hat. I carried the wrinkled envelope in my back pocket.

During the cab ride to the hotel the air was full of what I guess would be called Irish blarney. The hotel, a nice old standard with high ceilings and bellmen with red cheeks and wide Irish smiles who always seemed to have a poem on their lips, was pleasant enough. My small room had a bed piled so high with Irish linen and lace that as I sat, my feet dangled over the edge and couldn't touch the carpet. A quick change of clothes and I was out the door. My pocket contained the letter from Top Hat.

I asked a few questions and found that Grafton Street was an easy walk from the hotel and was at the heart of the central shopping district in downtown Dublin.

By the time I had emerged from the hotel the sun was making an impressive entrance as the clouds dispersed. The air was clear and inviting and ripe with the delicate scent of damp tree leaves and flower beds. The sun provided an accent to the conversation of elements, making the afternoon stroll breathtakingly beautiful. The short walk to Grafton Street took me past countless pubs and eateries, and private residences that were crammed together like old library books.

In twenty minutes I arrived at the top of a very busy Grafton Street. Someone told me later that when the sun comes out, the doors of Dublin open, and the people come out as well.

The street had been converted into a walking mall and was tightly lined with small boutiques and corporate retail outlets. It was populated with numerous outdoor food vendors selling everything from flowers to throw rugs. The place was alive with pedestrians. From corner to corner, there were international tourists, many coming from the all-in-one-price vacation ships anchored in the port a short distance away. It was a mob scene.

As I stood considering it all, cabs dropped off passengers at a curb nearby. These people had come to shop, all emerging from their cab smiling and happy at the prospect of cavorting with their credit cards.

A man nearby stood atop a small milk crate, shouting at those passing by about their faith, or apparent lack of it, and warning them of the evils of a consumer culture, while his cohorts distributed attractive leaflets offering simple salvation, available at three convenient locations nearby.

I headed up and down the street as I walked along to see if I could spot the Rat Catcher. The description of the man was a bit vague. Top Hat had said it wouldn't be hard to locate him: "Don't worry, man, the good Rat Catcher can't be found, he is to be discovered." Whatever that meant. "He's a man of rags and a slightly nasty demeanor. Look for him in the center of a circle defined by a red rope. Just listen for laughter, that's a sign that Rat Catcher is nearby." Top Hat had said this all with a smile.

Now, as I walked through this Irish shopping experience, I focused on spotting a red rope, which seemed to be the most singular of the clues.

My first encounter with a busker was a small man playing the Irish flute in front of an old furniture store. Like so many of the other buskers in European streets, he shared company with a couple of dogs that slept with disinterest at his feet. (I found out later that buskers who have friendly dogs get more tips from the audience.) The man played his flute with intensity and precision while only a handful of people looked on for a few short moments before being seduced back into a retail trance. I watched him for a couple of minutes and was wondering why more people weren't standing in awe of this man's talent. He could really play! But alas, few would share my enthusiasm for his ample musical abilities, preferring instead to stumble around in crowded stores.

After a couple of quick tunes, he put his flute down and picked up a guitar, which he played with equal talent.

Again, I was one of only a few people to stop and actually pay attention to this man's accomplished playing. The undertow of commerce was too strong for most to resist, and one by one those who paused were pulled back into the sea of shoppers.

I freed a couple of euros from my wallet and put them into his music case. "Cheers!" he said. "Cheers!" I continued on my way. This scene would repeat itself over and over as I walked the full length of Grafton. I would see buskers performing with vigor and talent but unable to capture the attention of the people passing by.

After I'd walked the entire length of the street, I came upon a man working a tall marionette puppet. The puppet was clad in black leather with handmade high-heeled shoes no longer than two inches each. Save for the strings, this puppet looked surprisingly like Tina Turner. A small boom box provided the Tina Turner soundtrack as the man, dressed from head to toe in black, manipulated the strings to animate the puppet to life. He was one of best puppeteers I'd ever seen, practiced and accomplished, and yet no one really paid much attention. I dropped some coins in his hat and continued on my way.

I'd been walking for a couple of hours and the noise and clamor had begun to take its toll. I was tired and wanted a bath, dinner, and an early bedtime. I strolled through the throng of people and made my way back up the retail stream to the head end of Grafton and my hotel.

As I approached the area where a couple hours earlier

the eager preacher had been trying to save the souls of shoppers, I noticed a rather large crowd laughing and applauding. I could hear them from some distance and at one point they gasped and then cheered loudly. I was interested, Rat Catcher or not. But I had a feeling I knew who was in the center of this circle of humanity.

The Red Rope

I approached the outer edge of the circle of people that had gathered to watch. I started to push myself forward through the dense crowd, occasionally catching a glance of a bald head and a small hat being tossed in the air. The crowd seemed to be transfixed, mesmerized by what was happening inside this large circle. The crowd was about eight to ten people deep and so dense that it took me a few minutes to make my way to a place where I could get an unobstructed view of what was happening. I stood watching this oddly dressed performer for a moment, wondering if this really was the infamous Rat Catcher whom Top Hat talked about. He certainly dressed the part.

I had reached the inner edge of the circle when my foot hit something that caused me to look down. There it was. I now knew for certain I was in the right place, for running along the front edge of my shoes, and circling the Rat Catcher, creating a space inside the crowd, was a red rope.

The Rat Catcher

In the center of the circle was a tall, thin man with a tiny hat perched on the top of his head. He was wearing baggy clothes and a ragged old fur vest. His clothes made him look huge and imposing. His face was lightly covered with dirt, and he had a salt-and-pepper beard. He looked like a vagrant, a vagrant on a rant. I could see the spark in his youthful green eyes, and though he looked old, grumpy, and ragged, his eyes betrayed something else. Underneath the gruff exterior was something far kinder and gentler than would first appear. It was one of the many contradictions that made his performance both compelling and curious.

His energy was nuclear, clear and focused. He had only a small suitcase of props to work with and otherwise seemed to find ample inspiration in the personal effects his audience carried with them; things like umbrellas, cameras, strollers, and shopping bags instantly became part of the show. The crowd seemed to trust him, letting him provoke and push them around. At one point he escorted a woman into the center of the circle, took off his hat in a gentlemanly fashion, and handed it to her. All the while he was wearing a Charlie Chaplin smile, and exuding a sober hobo's confidence. He reached and gently took her purse away, and slung it over his shoulder and instantly began to walk around the circle with a decidedly feminine swish to his hips, chin held high in a mock runway-model gait. The crowd howled when he stopped, turned to face her, and struck a pose as if on the cover of a fashion magazine. Applause.

Rat Catcher walked up to another woman who was sharing the spotlight with him, and stood with his back to her back and began to lean into her, back to back, pushing gently, and acting as if he was a flirtatious boyfriend getting cozy with her. While he was doing this, he began to look in her purse, occasionally peering over his shoulder and sporting a Cheshire grin of transparent guilt. Of course the woman knew he was digging in her purse but made no attempt to steal it back, choosing instead to laugh and play it all up.

Rat Catcher walked over to his prop suitcase, which was perched flat atop a cement garbage receptacle. He pulled out a cloth, covered the top of the suitcase, and then proceeded to dig through her purse again, only this time he started pulling items out one by one and setting them atop the cloth-covered suitcase. He managed to finesse a laugh out of each and every item he extracted. He used her makeup, stole the coins from her wallet, did a magic trick with one of her dollar bills, wrote out a check to himself, and handed out all of her credit cards to children standing in the audience (quickly taking them back while admonishing them for stealing).

His biggest laugh came when he looked deep into her purse and seemed shocked by something he'd discovered. He quickly picked up a tin bucket that was sitting near some other props, set it on the suitcase, and then began to pull out individually wrapped candies. He dropped them one by one into the bucket, and this continued for what seemed like minutes. Just when we thought he was finished finding candy, there was more, and more; literally handfuls of wrapped sweets. The laughter grew louder as the candies seemed to come from some bottomless source. No sooner were the candies relieved of their place in the pit of her purse, when he pulled out a couple of apples, an orange, and two bananas. Then there were coins, pennies mostly, which he seemed to extract by the handfuls. It all ended when he pulled out a large quartz rock, which he dropped into the bucket with a loud clunk. By this time the bucket was full of coins, candy, fruit, and the quartz. The crowd cheered loudly.

At that point a man with a camera standing on the edge of the circle took a small step forward to get a photograph of the Rat Catcher and his new purse-carrying partner. When he stepped forward, he tripped lightly on the leg of a small boy seated on the ground in front of him. As he stumbled into the circle, the Rat Catcher quickly ran over and caught him with a melodramatic flair. Once the man had regained his balance, all the while laughing very hard, the Rat Catcher ordered him back into the circle.

Rat Catcher then turned to the rest of the crowd, with his back to the cameraman, and displayed a nice gold watch in his hand. After some curious laughter, Rat Catcher turned and asked the cameraman what time it was. The man looked at his wrist only to realize that his watch was missing. "Hey! That's my watch!" he boomed. Rat Catcher smiled, and then held up the watch for everyone to see. The crowd cheered as the man came to get his watch, laughing and enjoying every moment of it.

Rat Catcher finally took a bow as the crowd cheered. He offered words of wisdom to encourage the ample number of onlookers to put a spot of money in his hat or bucket, telling them this was his livelihood and that while smiles and laughter were indeed an important part of their participation in his show, the "hat-pass" was, in fact, the most important part of this audience participation. After a final round of applause the crowd slowly dispersed, with many of them lining up to give him money and to take a picture with him.

"Ladies and gentlemen, if you find giving a particular pleasure, please indulge your pleasures!"

Everyone was smiling.

"Folks, just remember the last time you paid eight euro to see a movie, and it wasn't so good. Hey, I wasn't that good either, so give me four!"

The crowd of willing donors was quite large and Rat Catcher took his time, chiding the group continually in a humorous attempt to get more money in his hat.

"This, ladies and gentlemen, is the only way I make my living. Other than paid endorsements, my full-time job, consulting, writing books, and being on television, this is it!" Some in the crowd groaned with laughter as they waited for their turn to get a picture.

All of it was over in a matter of a few short minutes and Rat Catcher was busy putting away his props. He dumped his hat money in a pillowcase that was already sagging under the weight of "gifts" from a previous show. It was time for me to introduce myself and give him the envelope that Top Hat had sent along. I stepped over to him as he continued to put his props away into the suitcase.

Brushed Off

"You must be Rat Catcher?" I asked.

"Rumor, all rumor," he said while putting away the fruit he had produced during the purse routine.

"Oh, well, I thought you fit the description of Rat Catcher that this performer in London had described to me. He said you'd be in baggy rag clothes, that you'd have the biggest crowds, and that you were the best of the best," I said, hoping the compliment would convince him to warm up to me.

"Who would say such awful things about me?" he said with a noncommittal smile.

"He calls himself Top Hat, and he—"

"The Hat told you to look me up?" He stopped to look at me intently. "I haven't heard from him in a while. We met at Piccadilly way back. We moved over to Covent Garden for a couple years until it got too crowded with performers. He doesn't perform anymore, you know; he's a gentleman."

"Yeah, that's what he said. Anyway, the Hat asked me to give you this envelope, told me not to open it and that it was very important, that you'd know what to do with it." I handed Rat Catcher the tattered envelope. He turned it over and studied it carefully.

"Yeah, I know what it is. All of us here know what it is," he said, putting it into his coat pocket. "Thanks." He shut the lid of his suitcase and was getting ready to leave.

"Listen, I was wondering if I might buy you a cup of coffee. Top Hat said you like to drink lots of coffee, and I'd like to find out more about what you do."

"That's nice, but I've got another show in forty-five minutes and then I've got plans for the evening. Sorry, but thanks for delivering the envelope, and would you give the Hat my best when you see him?" He stuck his hand out to shake mine.

"Sure, I'll pass on your good wishes," I said. I shook his hand, after which he put on his hat, grabbed his suitcase, and melted into the crowd.

Well, that didn't end the way I thought it would. I found the Rat Catcher and he blew me off. I think the Hat did say something about the Rat Catcher's quirks?

I stood for a moment in the middle of the pedestrian mayhem. There were hordes of people clogging the streets; the din of their conversations created a gentle white noise as background. I could hear an Irish flute nearby, and farther off in the distance an opera singer stood on a corner singing Italian lyrics. There was energy on this street, so many people smiling, chatting with friends or lovers who were sharing the experience.

As I stood off to one side and took it all in, I thought about how the Rat Catcher would stand in the middle of this chaos and find a focus, and how the audience voluntarily and nervously gathered in a circle around him. He was able to command attention, lead them, and without much effort, convince some of them to stand in front of a couple hundred people and be his performance partners.

There was an empty bench near the corner of Grafton and Wicklow Streets and I took a seat. I thought about my life in sales and all the years I'd spent crafting and fine-tuning my "sales presentation." *My sales presentation bores me. I wonder if it bores those I give it to?*

I have always been aware of how I dress and carry myself with my peers. I am even more aware of the image I present to a client. Everything I do at work, whether with client or co-worker, has elements of a performance embedded in it. But mine was a performance style I now questioned after seeing a very different kind of performance. I would love to have available the energy provoked by the Rat Catcher. It certainly wouldn't be boring!

As I thought about Rat Catcher, and many of the other buskers I had watched today and at Covent Garden, I realized I had seen something genuine. What stood out wasn't the refinement of the act, but more how they showed up when they performed.

I'd mastered the art of disciplined selling; I did it by the numbers. I was a winner, but there was something missing for me at the core of it all, something lacking in my relationship to my work, to others, and even to myself. The buskers who attracted the biggest crowds had an authenticity I increasingly lacked. I needed the Rat Catcher to explain to me how he did what he did.

I remembered my first job working in the toy department of a large department chain. I loved that job, because I could play with kids and their parents, showing them the latest have-to-have-it toy. There was always energy in that job; even when kids were pitching a fit over something, I was able to engage them with toys and turn the encounter into something energetic and fun. In college, I worked in a bookstore and was always so energized by all the knowledge on the shelves and people coming to find something interesting to read.

There was a sense of freedom in those jobs, because the customers and I were urgently and mutually in need of each other. Now there are more expectations, more to lose and yet more to gain. There are politics and power struggles; there is the unending competition and drive for innovation and change. As I work to expand my sales contacts and improve my performance I call on people who don't want to see me or simply don't want to be bothered, much less buy, or they simply want to buy what they buy without seeing me at all. And yet my success depends on finding a way to help new clients see that what Jensen has to offer could benefit their patients, and help existing clients learn about new products.

The Rat Catcher, it would seem, had few obstacles in the way of his performance. But he also had to contend with a chaos and type of competition that would destroy most businesspeople. Is it possible that what I could learn from these performers is the secret of focus, how to make more compelling presentations, and the source of the energy that fuels it all? I needed to investigate my questions, and I became even more convinced as I sat anonymously on the bench swallowed by the rush of people that my answers could be found along the breathing edge of the circle of humanity surrounding the Rat Catcher.

I can't let it drop here. I have to find this guy again and learn what there is to learn. Top Hat had a reason for sending me here. After all, my life has been built around persistence, and now it seems the pursuit is worth the effort. He can't be hard to find, and once I do, I'll wait and watch for my opportunity to make another connection. If I can sell to doctors and hospital purchasing agents, I can sell a man in rags on a free cup of coffee! Or can I?

Rat Catcher Round Two

He wasn't aware of my presence as I waited. I stayed at a distance until he managed to gather a crowd. Once he began his show, I snuck into the anonymity of the group and watched him work. I didn't want him to know I was there. At one point, he was doing some tricks with his hat, when he suddenly tossed it over the crowd and it landed on me. I picked it up and tossed it back, and I knew then that he was very much aware of my presence.

The show ended, and he rolled right into collecting money from the audience for the performance, making them laugh and keeping their attention as a long line of people walked over and filled his hat with money. I took a brief stroll and sat on a bench a short distance away, and waited. As he rolled up the red rope and prepared to leave the area, I approached him again.

"Hey. I'm the guy that gave you the envelope from Top Hat, and I was—"

"This was my last show for the day and I'm a bit burned up, plus I've got some errands to run and need to eat, so why don't you find me later."

"Sure . . . sure, I'll look forward to it." I waited for a few moments and started to tag along at a distance. He stopped and greeted several people. In fact, it seemed he knew everyone along the way.

I followed him and eventually he entered a restaurant. The sign on the outside of the place was a big top hat, turned upside down and full of money. Large red letters surrounded the money-filled hat—MADD HATTERS, it said. There were some tables and chairs outside, and many more inside. It was a noisy place, with cement floors, a loud refrigerator compressor, and Broadway music playing through the sound system.

I went inside and sat down, but I did not see the Rat Catcher anywhere. *I wonder if he has given me the slip again. May as well have something to eat and drink.*

Round Three

I ordered a pint with my fish and chips and waited. Rat Catcher wasn't there, but there were other street performers I recognized. They sat at a table on the other side of the small dining area. All were laughing and carrying on, telling stories about a crazy person in the audience or something about a "pitch," a term I had never heard used in that way before.

He showed up just as I got my food, not coming through the front door, but emerging from the kitchen, talking to a couple of the servers. He headed over to the table where the other performers sat. They all started talking with great animation, polishing off more than a few pints as the noise level rose.

I felt awkward just being there. As he walked into the main room he looked around and made no movement or indication that he recognized me at all. I decided I would finish my food and head back to the hotel. The ongoing conversation in my head started again.

This is ridiculous. I'm a business guy with a good job.

Every job has its pitfalls. Chasing a street performer is probably a waste of time.

I recognized Rat Catcher's laugh. Looking over at the table where he was sitting, I saw him finishing up a magic trick that involved a lighter, the tablecloth, and a cigarette. The buskers were each countering with different punch lines, or standing up to act out some kind of physical interpretation of the same joke or routine.

This is how they shared and expanded their work, I thought. *They would casually try things out for the group. There wasn't secrecy over material and routines they created; they valued the exchange of ideas, and they were open, each trying to help the other find the best combination of word and action that would result in the biggest impact. It was a cooperative effort.*

In my work I've always believed in helping the new guys out. At the same time I worried they might be too good at what they do. Heaven knows I've made a healthy living selling, but at times I felt more like I was chasing a lifestyle than a life.

"Hello, Jim."

I looked up to see the man himself standing by my table.

"May I sit down?"

"For sure. I have been following you around with one hope, that you might spend a moment or two with me."

"Ah-ha, you have an agenda!" His face lit up as he looked at me. "And you didn't give up. So! You didn't even know it, but you passed the test of the first envelope with flying colors. Your persistence shows that more than a whim motivates you. A lot of folks find us interesting or curious and would like to talk. But if we took time for anyone who asked, we would die of starvation."

"I can understand that. Did you say 'first envelope'?"

"Indeed I did, but more about that later. How much do you know about our little test?"

"Top Hat gave me some background on the envelope."

"Yes. It's just a little fun. First, another respected busker must refer you. Second, you must persist because the energy required to succeed must be natural. In other words, it must flow freely from within. And third, well, how can I be of service?"

It was a big question. Here I was with someone I was just getting to know, in a city I didn't know, talking about an approach to work and living that seemed equally far from home. What *did* I want?

Opening of the Envelope

My mind was spinning and I was tongue-tied. I took a deep breath and just started talking.

"I'm not sure where to begin." Not exactly knocking him dead with clarity. Then it came to me. "Ahh . . . I am really curious about the contents of the envelope."

"Easily done." And the Rat Catcher took out an envelope and carefully tore off one end, blowing into it to make it easier to access the treasure inside. He unfolded one sheet of typing paper. On the exposed side was a circle with a small dot in the middle. He turned it over to show me that the other side was blank. He said, "This is where you are," as he pointed to the blank page. "And this is where you need to be," he continued as he indicated the dot in the middle of the circle on the other side.

I hope I didn't look as stupid as I felt.

"You must approach this part of your journey as if you were a blank page. You might know a great deal about the specifics of what you do, but you must act as if you are a blank page when you consider a new way of being. The circle is the key."

I just stared at him.

"It's important that you not invite too much company along on the journey."

"Company?" I was obviously alone.

"You are accompanied by your need for quick answers and quick fixes, and the comfort of routine thinking. But by trying to make new ideas conform to old ways of thinking you will miss the 'juice.' So keep your margins wide and your options open. Remember, the 'juice' is in the 'jam,' not in routine. Hold that thought. Now, what is on your mind? Begin."

"Well, the issue on the top of my list is finding the energy I need for my work. Being a sales agent has become stale and way too predictable. I feel like I'm on autopilot, powered only by my discipline and ability to work long hard hours. Something fundamental is missing. I still deliver good results by doing what I have always done, but I feel like my energy and enthusiasm is slowly draining away and is not being replenished. I'm frantically treading water and the tide is getting stronger. It is harder and harder for me to stay in place, much less move forward. I work all the time. I'm burned-out and I worry about not being able to get out of bed one of these mornings, paralyzed by fear and boredom." Wow. I had certainly let it all out.

"I see," he said calmly. "You sell for a living?"

"Yes, I'm in sales. How did you know that?"

"You just told me, Jim. Continue."

I filled him in on my history with Jensen.

"So you're here at Hatters, talking with a strange busker, someone you've never met, looking for connections between what I do and what you do, in the hope that you can find a new source of energy to fuel your work? Is that about right?"

"Yep, that's about it. I suppose it's strange to have a businessperson trying to learn this from a street performer, I mean, what do you really know about business and what do I really know about being a busker?"

"Well, I don't want to ruin your thesis, Einstein, but I know quite a bit about business. Banking was my pitch for five years. Hard to believe today, but I worked as a bank teller at a small bank in Boulder, Colorado, where I grew up. My dad taught international business at the University of Colorado Business School. I grew up in Boulder and went to school at UC, majoring in finance."

"Finance?"

"Surprised?"

"Surprised and impressed. I didn't do well in the math courses. So how did you get here doing this?"

"I happened onto buskers while shopping at the Boulder Mall and became fascinated by what they did. Soon I was hanging out with the guys, kind of like a mascot. I would help them pass the hat and stuff. Then I learned a little magic, some stunts, and did a few little hat shows, to warm up the pitch for the big guns. I ended up doing this all the way through college and the income helped pay for my tuition. But I never thought of being a busker as a career.

"One day I realized I loved being a busker more than being a banker. That insight led to a change in my life. It took almost a year, but I eventually made the transition to full-time busker from bank teller."

He looked over to the table of performers. "Actually, most of these guys have had, or still have, straight jobs." He chuckled.

"It took that long to figure out you didn't want to be a banker?"

"Good point. There was a woman in the picture, of course. My girlfriend became my fiancée and her vision for me was distinguished banker. My parents were only too happy to reinforce that point of view, thinking it was indeed time for me to settle down to serious work. Life is interesting, isn't it?

"Anyway, I moved here about twelve years ago and for a while, even then, I had to work as a bartender and at other odd jobs to make ends meet."

I was more intrigued then ever. "I'm not sure why, but watching you work on the street, building on a theme with an audience, it's energizing. I guess I'm taken with the whole idea of buskers. I mean, you just stop in the middle of a busy street and set up your show."

"Our business location is the street corner."

"I need some of what you've got. I'm not sure how to put it exactly, but I need a fresh approach to what I do."

Natural Energy

"What you want is natural energy. And all I do is work with energy, so we should be able to figure something out," he said as he ordered up a cup of coffee and a snack.

"An audience comes to the circle, curious and hungry. They're curious about what is going on, why there is a crowd, and hungry to be delighted, surprised, or provoked. Not hard really. Your customers are probably just as hungry for something similar but a business mind-set usually screens out that possibility."

"Do you really think there are ideas that can translate to my work? There is a big difference between what you do and what I do for a living."

"Wow! No offense, but that's quite funny. Can energy translate! All any of us do is work with energy, you're no different. I mean, it is either work with 'energy' or 'discipline' in order to get things done. What would you prefer? A life fueled by natural energy or fifty push-ups?"

"The reason why I am here is that my success is built on a high level of discipline. I win by working harder and longer. And I can do a hundred push-ups."

"Let me see!"

By the time I reached the halfway point the other buskers were all crowded around cheering. When I reached a hundred I did one extra, to the delight of the buskers, and then I sat gasping in my chair and listening to the hoots and hollers. And I felt the energy. Not the energy of discipline it took to do a hundred push-ups, but a more natural sort of energy that flowed from the cheering buskers I had just provoked.

"Very impressive! I bet it took a lot of practice to get to that point."

I smiled. "That is what I do best. Push myself."

"Thankfully, there is another way. I think you have come to the right place. Buskers are experts on natural energy. We even have our own language of energy. All great buskers have to master energy. We rely entirely on volunteers to make a living. If no volunteers form a circle around us, we don't eat."

"I would like to find the busker in me and put it to work as soon as possible," I said.

"It can be done. I did it myself as a bartender. I did well because I brought the busker to work. I would interact with customers in the manner of a busker and the energy from those encounters and from my antics would attract others to the bar. Not a lot of tricks; I mostly worked with what my customers brought with them. You know, if I had brought the busker in me to the bank, I might still be a banker." He smiled and said, "Or in jail."

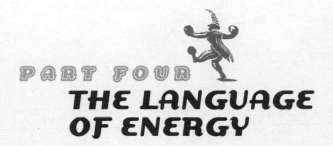

PART FOUR
THE LANGUAGE OF ENERGY

Claim Your Pitch

"There is a language the old-timers use and I think it would be worthwhile for you to learn it. The language will help you see the world more like a busker sees the world. Let's begin. See that guy over there with the wild hair?" The Rat Catcher pointed across the pub.

"Yes."

"That's Mephisto. He's a nasty bloke. He's funny, too, a bit on the blue side. Mephisto is in a good mood tonight because he did well today; he had a good pitch."

"You have used that word a few times now. The pitch I know is what a salesperson does in front of a client, give a pitch, or something to do with music. But how is it different in your world?"

"Our use of the word is not that much different from yours. To us, the pitch is the actual physical location chosen and also the energy generated by the location. So it is both a place, like a busy intersection, and the vibes we are sending when we take up residence in that place.

"The 'pitch' is a *place of possibilities*. When we are looking for a good pitch, we're looking for a place that has the elements needed to feed our circle. It is often found among the din, the distractions, and the messes. All the stuff of life is really material found in the best pitch.

"Think of the people you most like to work with, people that energize you. It's like you are on the same note, the same pitch. As a busker, my work is about setting the pitch, and having people gather because they hear it and they feel it. More often than not, my entire show is designed to get everybody on the same note by the end of the performance. It's like being the conductor for an orchestra, only it's not music I'm conducting, it's energy.

"Sometimes, a busker needs a smaller pitch, to do more intimate work. A sleight-of-hand magician needs close-up space, with less external distractions. We fine-tune our pitch to fit the needs of our material.

"So a busker calls the place he sets up his show, the pitch. A pitch is chosen to give the busker an advantage to claim the right foot traffic and the optimal local aesthetics. The busker's manner of presence in the pitch sets a tone as it is the busker's decision who he or she will be while present in the pitch. And the busker's attitude while in the pitch is his claim. Is that clear?"

"I think so. It is both where you are and who you are being there."

"Brilliant! Dedicate yourself to being mindful about **claiming your pitch,** and great things will follow."

A *"pitch"* is the place you perform and also the tone set by "who you are being while you are performing." Your attitude is your "claim."

Claim your pitch.

Juice the Jam

"This is such a different way of seeing the world," I said. "I've watched a lot of buskers over the past few days, and I still get kind of nervous seeing how far some of you will go to get the crowd involved, or to build a routine."

Rat Catcher smiled. "Yeah. You've got to know danger and vulnerability in this business; it's a key part of the equation. **Sometimes the juice is in the jam.**"

"The juice is in the jam?"

"Do I hear an echo?" The Rat Catcher paused to take a sip from his Madd Hatters mug.

"You know, when you get into a jam, you're stuck. When we work a pitch, it's like we look for the jam, for the obstacle, because a jam is always an energy source. The obstacle, the mistake, the random, the interesting, the complication, that's where we find the juice."

There was a thoughtful look on his face when he added, "The world is chaotic and full of crazy stuff; the guys here know the best performances are those where some unexpected stuff happens and you build on it.

"Someone falls, a cell phone rings, a siren goes off, a policeman walks up, a child cries, a heckler starts a diatribe or someone acts outlandishly; all of these things, when they happen, become the center of attention. A good busker welcomes these jams and works with them. They are called jams because you are in a jam and need to respond. The circle is curious about how you will handle the jam and there is a moment of truth. Handle it well and the energy flows. Handle it poorly and you can break the circle. If you can step into a jam and survive, the applause is always the loudest. You might be able to juggle twenty burning torches with your tongue, but the applause will be louder if you escape a jam with grace and bring the circle with you. That's why the most successful buskers aren't the most talented; they are the best juicers."

He paused for a moment to look back over to the other table of his performing friends.

"Do you mean my best material may not be planned and isn't necessarily under my control?"

He looked back. "That is it in a nutshell, Jim. We buskers look at anything that happens as material from which to build our success. You can resist the jam or you can work with it. If you resist it, you lose energy. If you work with it, you will attract and release energy."

"So if someone misses an appointment, I spill coffee on my shirt, or we have a massive recall on a drug, that it is all material," I said.

"Yes! Once any of those things happens you can't make it un-happen. That is the jam. Now, you can work with it or you can run away and hide under your desk, but you can't hide the jam, because it is there for all to see. You need to **juice that jam**.

"Remember, Jim, we are performers, not actors. When you're working as an actor, say on some stage in the West End, it is different. You really don't want chaos. Yet even in the West End when a baby cries or a cell phone rings, the best actors make a witty comment that flows from their character and then continue with the script unperturbed. Any other approach creates negative energy and tension in the audience. The audience is more upset because of empathy for the actor than for themselves, and a good actor understands that he or she needs to relieve the tension.

"In fact, my best ideas always come out of something unexpected. The new idea that later becomes a form of insurance often emerges from a glitch, mistake, flub, catcall, or unplanned event.

"When you're on the street, it's the other way around; the audience is the show whether they know it or not. Seeing everyone as a collaborator changes the relationship. I've been doing this a long time now and I recognize that while I may not create the jam, I can almost always use the jam for juice." He was on a roll.

"Tell me something. Are the people you call on passive observers or potential collaborators? Would your customers rather be engaged in a discussion or would they prefer to be ignored while you give them a formal presentation? Where do you find more energy, in the back row listening to a speech or in the front row having a conversation?"

"You know I have always considered a formal presentation as the professional way to approach a customer," I replied. "I realize that it may simply be a safe way for me to attempt to control everything. You are helping me see that it may not be the most effective way to work with a client and that not everything can or should be controlled. I think my clients would say my presentations are professional and also admit they were bored to death. How can my clients not be bored? *I'm* bored.

"And things do happen that are not planned. Always! And to ignore them and continue as if they had not happened is something I am now questioning."

 A *"jam"* is the uncontrolled and unexpected, anything that happens without warning whenever a group of human beings assemble.

A "jam" is welcome because it provides a source of novelty and provocation, and novelty and provocation always produce a burst of natural energy, the "juice."

A "jam" calls on all your skills as a street performer as you must engage the jam in order to access the energy. Every "jam" is different. The rewards are huge when you skillfully handle a jam.

Hence, the "juice" is in the "jam."

Juice the jam.

Mine the Mess

"If that is the case, Jim, you desperately need to learn to work with the jam," the Rat Catcher said emphatically. "Success for me comes when I investigate the obstacles, look under the rocks, and explore the novel. It might make you more interesting to your prospects and it will surely make you more interesting to yourself. And if you don't have a jam, you can always look to the mess for ideas."

"The mess?

"Yes, Jim, another scientific busker term, only this is one I created! The 'mess' is both a way of looking at the world and a way of acting. Sometimes I will stand on top of a garbage can as a way to open a pitch. Slowly I will remove the contents and scatter them around. In busy places, these cans are emptied often and so I don't run much of a risk by handling the contents, but those who watch deal with the image of garbage and are both repulsed and attracted. They are curious and move toward me. The mess gives me all the material I need.

"Other times I will empty a purse and play with the contents. Think of how children play with their box of toys. They don't just pull out one toy at a time; they dump the whole box out so they have more options to choose from. It's no different for me. Get all the stuff out in the open, and you can imagine the amazing possibilities that emerge."

"I think some of those things emerge from your pocket, like the fruit I saw you locate in a woman's purse," I said.

"Nothing wrong with a little trickery for insurance, Jim."

"Insurance? You mentioned that before. What is insurance?"

"All in good time, Jim. We'll get to that in a minute. But before I explain insurance I want to double-check and make sure you fully understand the 'mess.' All around you is material just waiting to be used. It is always there. It may be the contents of your briefcase, the personality of the client, a recent event in your life, or your imagination. Whereas a jam is something unexpected that confronts you, a mess is something you call upon when needed. Tell me what you must do with this mess."

After a thoughtful pause, I looked directly at Rat Catcher and said, "You need to *mine the mess*, for its energy."

"Excellent! And what might be an example from your world of sales?"

"When I'm in someone's office, there are objects on the desk, along with pictures and books. When a book is on the desk it is either being read or is meant to impress. It can be picked up, mentioned directly, referred to indirectly or ignored. Sometimes there are motivational posters on the wall and occasionally there are degrees or awards proudly framed for all to see. I always notice when there is a gym bag in the corner."

"Good. You are seeing the world through the eyes of a busker. It is all material with which to work creatively." The Rat Catcher leaned back in his chair, balancing on the back legs. "Jimmy. You've watched me and others work our pitch and mine the mess. What connects with you?"

"There is a great deal that looks helpful. Perhaps I'm just a business dude who thought he always wanted to be an artist, or a performer. Sales seemed to be a good way to use the communication skills that seemed so natural to me. And it has provided me with a good living. But I think it *would* be more fun if I could find a way to engage more fully with my customer. Perhaps I mean engage more fully with the world. The idea that everything is material is both freeing and a bit frightening."

"You've got that right, Jim. I know what office life *can* be like, but that doesn't mean it has to be that way. If you want to know what it means to work with danger or to discover freedom in the midst of the conformity, you've got to take some risks." He stopped for a moment to consider what he was saying. "And the energy that flows from that place is natural energy. The unscripted kind."

"I heard someone say once in a speech that you need to 'live out loud,' and I really didn't understand what she meant. You guys clearly live out loud. And I think a part of living out loud is welcoming all of life on its own terms and not trying to control everything. I want to live out loud. I want to live out loud at work and I want to live out loud in life," I said.

"Yeah, loud is one of my best qualities! The fun for me in this line of work is the day-to-day discoveries I find in my audience. I feel like an explorer sometimes, or a scientist. When I'm out there on the street working with a crowd, I'm trying to stir the pot, or better yet, kick the damn thing over. You'll never really know what's inside something until you risk the mess of dumping it out. Sometimes what you randomly find has the most energy," he said, pounding on the table.

"So, Jim, it is more than just accepting the unexpected and embracing the ebb and flow of life. It is also provoking life to see what you can uncover from the ever-present messes."

The mess can be found in a briefcase, a purse, a shopping bag, a photo album, or a garbage can overflowing with effluvium. What makes it a mess is that it isn't ordered and it is a source of endless discovery. When the mess is embraced, each item brings novelty, attracts curiosity, and releases energy. You may not always have a jam, but there is always a mess if you just remember to look for it.

Remember, the mess is chock full of the material needed for a top performance in sales, service, and in life. Since life is a mess, a mess is always near at hand.

Mine the mess.

Develop Insurance

"**N**ow, let me tell you about insurance," the Rat Catcher continued. "It is a small but important topic. We all prepare for the time when nothing seems to be working by having insurance to fall back on. And I don't mean life insurance, although it might be a form of health insurance. Without it, I would not be healthy. I wouldn't eat and I might get attacked by the crowd!"

"So insurance is something you can fall back on, something that is practiced and effective in a pinch."

"At a pitch or in a pinch; we all need insurance and you, Jim, have the spirit of a busker. Your insurance may be the way you handle a mess you carry with you and call on when you need energy, or it may be a routine, an interaction, or a gimmick."

"So the magically appearing fruit that you found in the woman's purse is a form of insurance. You know it will get a laugh and release energy, because you have done it many times before."

"Exactly. My insurance consists of a little magic, as

you saw, a routine or bit that is tried and true and always works with the audience. I think of insurance the same way I think of lighting a match, and I see the audience as the fuse waiting to be lit. After years of working in the streets, I've discovered and refined enough insurance that I now have many books of matches. The audience always has the fuse ready to be lit. We call it curiosity. In your work you, too, need to **develop insurance**."

"I think I do a little of that already," I said. "I hate being late, but there are some events for which you can't prepare and so once in a while I arrive late. To establish a relaxed atmosphere after we all get settled, I sometimes use a little hyperbole. For instance, I might say, 'A football team picked up my car as part of their training exercise and when the wheels were back on the ground I had lost ten minutes.' Of course, I use the name of the local team. Or I might say, 'Sorry, my wife just had sextuplets. Well, actually I am not married, but I had time to meet a woman, get married, and have children during the horrendous traffic jam I was a part of on the freeway. Does that happen often?'"

"Great example of insurance, Jim."

"Insurance" is what you can fall back on when you are short of material or simply draw a blank. You use insurance to light the fuse of curiosity in your audience, your prospect, your class, or your customer.

Insurance can be a tried-and-true crowd pleaser or a way of experimenting with vulnerability and experimentation. A top performer recognizes that authenticity is the world's best insurance. One genuine question is worth a hundred practical answers.

Develop your insurance.

Choose Your Close

"As buskers, we have another term that corresponds to a basic sales principle. We call it the 'close.'"

"You are correct. We talk endlessly about closing in sales," I said.

"There is, however, a subtle difference between our uses. You refer to getting the business. We refer to finishing the performance on a high note so when we pass the hat it comes back full of money. That is why a close may often contain some insurance. The better the close, the heavier the hat."

"So what is your best close?"

"My best closes come from the interaction. There is a sense of time and attention span that becomes internalized. So a bell goes off in my head when I am approaching the limit of my audience's attention. If what I am engaged in is high energy, I make that the close. When necessary I can draw on insurance for the close. I have a couple of tried-and-true closes."

"Was the random arrangement of people one of those closes?"

"You saw that, did you? Must have been that first time I saw you. Yes, that was insurance and that was a tried-and-true close. I take members of the audience and distribute them around the circle. I ask them to pretend they are money trees. Then I skip around and pick the fruit and when I get to the last person I take off through the crowd only to come back immediately and tell the trees they have the option of removing the money from my hat or feeling good about helping a busker make a living. It is all done in a lighthearted way and leads to a big hat.

"Another close I favor is to break the circle and to use the red rope as a starting line. Then I arrange the audience members in a number of straight lines, having a bit of fun while I do so, and all the while implying something great is about to happen. I then go to the front of the lines and hold out my hat. I suggest that we are engaged in improvisation and the next action is theirs to take."

"I think that is a bit more aggressive than I could ever be."

"Perhaps, but are you sure? What if you simply said, 'Does anyone want to buy some drugs?'" the Rat Catcher asked.

"I'm not sure I could do that. But it would certainly be different."

"Don't you think everyone in the conference room, auditorium, or office knows your ultimate objective?"

"Yes, that is all a part of our dance."

"Well, change the music once in a while, Jim. Take a

chance. It is the only way you can learn what is effective. The main difference between your world and my world is that your world is expected to be 'professional.' And 'professional' may be the biggest mess to mine. You develop your insurance by trying new things and your most important form of insurance is your close. Use your best judgment, but breathe some life into your close and you will bring some energy into your life."

"I have an idea."

"Great. Are you going to share?"

"Well, the difficult thing in closing is often making the transition from what is being discussed to a request for the business. What if I took a pair of white gloves with me and when it was time, I put on the white gloves meticulously as a way of signaling the change. I might play with that idea."

"That's the way a busker thinks, Jim."

 A "*close*" is the last thing you do before you "pass the hat." The particular close you choose must be selected carefully and be based on what you have learned during the presentation or performance. Choose your close wisely. A successful close will quite likely contain some insurance and great closes often become insurance.

Choose your close.

Pass the Hat

"A busker has one of the most clearly accountable professions on the planet. When we pass the hat at the end of a show our feedback is instantaneous. You kind of have an idea before you pass the hat. For instance, if there is no one left in the circle, it probably didn't go that well. There is a wonderful reciprocity in passing the hat and the energy is natural. We have no power and our customers give voluntarily. The hat-pass is a seamless part of the close; they work together. When you ask for the business, you are **passing the hat**. Hopefully you are following a great close and the hat will come back full.

"In your world of sales, the passing of the hat and the close are often confused. We keep them separate because without a great close you will have an empty hat. Closing does not always mean asking for the business. Closing is wrapping things up in a clear and compelling manner. Passing the hat is the request for something more. In your case, it is a request for an order, and in my case the request for a few quid."

"Passing the hat" is the only way a busker gets paid, but it is more than that. If it were just about money, it would be called "collecting tips" or "getting the money." Instead a more folksy term is used.

Passing the hat is feedback, a way to measure the magnitude of the natural energy released.

We all pass the hat in our own way, whatever our profession. We all have a bond with our customers, clients, colleagues, and family and need their objective feedback to gauge our performance. No matter how they say you did or how you think you did, you find out for real when you pass the hat.

Pass the hat.

Build a Circle

"You have really captured my imagination. But I know my time with you is short, so I want to ask you about one other thing," I said.

"One more subject works for me."

"Inside the envelope you opened, an envelope that looked cleaner than the one I gave you from Top Hat, was a piece of paper with a circle with a dot in the middle. I get that I am the dot. What does the circle represent?"

"I so hoped you would ask about that, Jimmy, and good for you for noting the switch. The circle represents the audience, but more importantly, the circle represents the natural energy that is there for you to use."

"I'm intrigued."

"Do you remember the man that stepped forward with his camera to get a picture?"

"Yeah, he tripped on a kid sitting on the ground and stumbled into the circle," I answered.

"Right. Well, that's an interesting case in point. He wanted a picture, and he was safe in the midst of the crowd. In a way the crowd itself is conformity, 'cause they just stand there and laugh and do what all the rest are doing. But this guy, he goes to take a picture and trips on some groundling and in a snap of a finger, he's the center of attention." At that the Rat Catcher snapped his long, bony fingers.

"In a little way, that's a lesson. He took the risk to get the picture and something interesting happened. He could have run back into the safety of the group, but he chose to stay inside the circle and let me humiliate and punish him for his misdeed, and the audience loved it. That man might have never been the attention of so many people, but for a few minutes this afternoon, he was the star of the show. And for me he was a source of natural energy.

"And you noted the way I defined my pitch?"

"A red rope," I said.

"And the rope formed a . . . ?"

"A circle."

"Exactly. When I claim my pitch, it is a matter of faith that I will eventually have a circle. As people assemble behind the rope they become the circle. The rope now has new meaning and I work to bring the circle closer to me as the gig continues.

"Let me see how well you have been listening. What do we call what happened when he fell into the center of the circle?"

"A jam. He created a jam. You could pretend it didn't happen and ignore the incident, but the focus is all on this guy and there is energy there to be explored."

"Exactly. We embrace life as it happens. There is no resistance, only material. We can choose to accept the material or let it go. Obviously, part of being successful as a busker is knowing what to choose and when.

"And how might I have created a mess similar to the jam if no one happened to fall into the circle?"

"You could have bumped someone, asked a woman to volunteer a man, taken someone's hat off and placed it in the middle, asked for someone who has a birthday, and if no one volunteers choose someone and say it doesn't have to be today."

"You may have a place on the street, Jimmy. And if one of the messes I make really works well?"

"Then it could become insurance and even be used as a close."

"You understand the language well, mate. Remember, the show inside the circle is just life, temporary. We performers get to create magic in the moment. We multiply the energy of our audience, knowing full well that it will never happen the same way again. We all know that the show ends, but if we're really good, if our good energy is multiplied, we have created something special in that moment.

"That's life, that's any job, that's any person anywhere. When they come to the edge of the circle, they are all equal and all of them, in some little way, are children waiting to see the magician create something amazing. And as performers we get to create something extraordinary, something the audience really loves but they probably couldn't describe, they just feel it, want it, and are uplifted by it in that moment. It's one of our little secrets."

The Rat Catcher was smiling in a way that was different from any expression I had seen on him before. It was a smile anchored in a deep wisdom and his eyes were burning into me.

"So, the audience comes to the edge of the circle to watch you and they get engaged, you pass the hat, and that's cool. What do you have that the audience wants so much?" I asked in a hushed tone that matched the mood.

The Rat Catcher chuckled a little, his eyebrow raised a bit, as if lifting the curtain on the light behind his eyes. His answer caught me by surprise.

"**Freedom!** There is nothing so compelling as being a witness to someone who is free. There is nothing so attractive as freedom. If you remember nothing else, remember this: Freedom and natural energy can't be separated, and it is the same for all of us. The audience is free to stay, to leave, to laugh or not, and the performer is free to act uninhibited. A performer who claims his or her freedom is powerful and attractive. It is universal. We all in some way honor the courage we know it takes for someone to claim their freedom in a world with too many rules."

We sat in silence for a moment. I knew the minute Rat Catcher said "freedom" that it was indeed true, and the idea would affect me for the rest of my life. There is nothing so engaging as someone who has claimed her or his freedom.

"So can this circle exist anywhere there are people?"

"Yes! The circle can be a performer's circle or it can be as big as the globe, as large as an office building, and as small as a wedding band. Family, co-workers, customers, and friends all form the circles of life.

"What is true about any circle is that there is an energy source to rally around, some common interest or idea that lives at the center of the circle. That can be a busker with a torch and chain saw, or it can be faith, marriage, an ideology, a corporate vision, or a new product presentation. To build a circle of energy there must be something compelling at the center."

The Rat Catcher continued, his energy building. "In the early days of mankind the center of the circle was a campfire or a storyteller. The busker, the sales agent, the teacher, and the service provider have replaced the fire and the storyteller."

"So the circle could also be a customer circle, a sales circle, a team circle, or a company circle?" I asked. "A circle is a way to discuss the vast energy potential when human beings congregate and interact. I think that is what Top Hat was telling me when he said I don't need to work alone, and by working alone I would always be limited."

"Oh, you're on to it, Jimmy."

The Rat Catcher paused for a moment. The din of the restaurant had picked up. The kitchen and bar were humming. He raised his hand and a pint was on the way. Then he continued. "The circle is like chemistry class in school. There are all these jars with various elements.

The elements by themselves aren't very interesting, but stir them together and it can get interesting real quick, right?" he said, laughing.

"People are kind of like that, only more volatile. In chemistry you have a table of elements and the predictable traits of the elements. The elements of our world are people and they are far less predictable. Buskers know that the audience is, shall I say, a renewable energy source!"

I thought about how so many salespeople work to become heavy "closers." They study and learn techniques on how to decipher a buyer's signals and clues so that they can "eliminate the objections" and get the ink on the bottom of the contract, and in the process they lose sight of what's really going on right under their nose. I also recognized that I'd become something of a selling automaton, leaning on my expertise at closing, running my routines of supersalesperson, and all the while missing the opportunities to connect in a meaningful and lasting way with my customers.

"When the Hat said I worked alone, he nailed it. I can see that when you work alone, you don't have access to the natural energy of the circle. You might make a buck, but you are just doing a shtick. And that shtick will soon grow old."

"Exactly. There are a lot of buskers who make a marginal living by doing a shtick. They may be quite talented, but they never take the risks of engagement necessary to feel the energy of the circle, to connect to the present moment. They think over everything in their heads first. They plot and plan each move, and seek to control and harness all the variables that give them a false sense of security. They try to manage what they don't really understand, and as a result they choke the energy out of their performances. They are not connected to their customers; they are doing something *to* their customers. And customers can feel the difference and they respond differentially when it is time to pass the hat.

"The best performers know that 'discovery' is a key element in building the energy of the circle. Even buskers with a routine and a script can elevate the level of their material, simply by remaining present to the audience and the environment. There is something to be discovered even in scripts and routines. The audience is fascinated by the potential of something unique happening. The audience comes because they don't know how it's going to end. Each thing the performer does increases curiosity and tension. When something novel happens, the sense of discovery releases energy because the audience has a part in its creation."

The Rat Catcher paused and looked at the ceiling for a moment.

"Jim, the circle is **natural energy**. Every person in the circle is a volunteer. This isn't something mystical or some kind of New Age magic, it's just human energy being exchanged."

Early storytellers sat by the campfire, their practiced words falling on the eager ears of those who formed a circle.

Court jesters and fools in the Middle Ages sat at the feet of kings and built their circles by broaching subjects the average person avoided for fear of losing a body part.

To build a circle, find a pitch, take a stand for freedom, authentically engage others, be vulnerable, draw on your abundant imagination, and treat what happens as precious material from which to extract energy.

Build a circle.

"I like the language of energy and see lots of uses, but I have a few more questions I want to ask before you leave."

"No."

"No?"

"Our time is up."

"Our time is up?" I asked.

"My office hours are over, Jimmy. I'll leave any loose

threads to the gentleman we call the Hat. It is time to celebrate and I will be rejoining my mates now. You are welcome to join us now that you are one of us."

"I hope the Hat will give me some more time."

"Did he ask you to look him up when you came back to London?"

"Yes."

"That's the way it works. You are one of us now, a part of the family. We have an investment in you. And even if the Hat doesn't have all the answers you seek, I think you owe him some feedback. You know, passing the hat, closure, results, information."

"Of course. I guess I have outstayed my welcome. Please forgive me."

"You haven't outstayed your welcome. You are *about* to outstay your welcome. So get the hell out of here and reclaim your life, mate. Oh. And take the original envelope back to the Hat. I guess you know not to open it."

After saying thank-you in a dozen ways, buying a round for the table of buskers, and enduring some good-natured ribbing and another request for push-ups, I started to leave. I was only a few feet from the raucous table when I heard my name. "Jim! Just a minute, Jim."

I turned around to see the Rat Catcher standing on a chair. He looked at me and at the now quiet group around the table.

"Jim, you have helped me clarify something important. I have often wondered about buskers who become very polished but can't fill a hat. I now think they suffer from the same malady that brought you here. They are no longer present in their pitch. They are doing a routine, a shtick. And when you are no longer present for your work, you are indeed alone, for you are not engaged with the world around you. It is when that happens that you slowly lose the life energy you need for sustenance and renewal. I want to honor you and bid you God-speed."

And all the buskers stood on their chairs and cheered as I turned and left for the hotel and the bags that needed packing.

Contemplating a
New Life at Work

On the short trip from Dublin to London, I engaged in my favorite pastime, a little daydreaming. I dreamt that I lived in a world that was all black and white. The landscape was black-and-white charts, reports, meetings, P&Ls, Power Point presentations, conference calls, bullet points, and deadlines. Everything was right or wrong, good or bad, black or white. Then at the end of my dream, my world became a world of vibrant color and I felt a sense of excitement and a deep peacefulness.

I woke up thinking that there wasn't a thing wrong or corrupt with how I've been living at work. It even allowed me to accumulate some pretty toys. But just perhaps the energy spent pursuing more synthetic goals had outpaced the value of the investment. I decided I wanted to live more fully, regardless of the price. I wanted to live in vivid colors, not shades of gray.

The street performers I'd met on my journey were junkies for the juice in the present moment. As a group they suffer the same maladies of being human that we all do: dysfunctional relationships, addictions, disorganization, and a host of physical challenges. What is different is that when they start performing, they gain an access to the embedded, natural energy in the relationship with the audience; there is reciprocity. Once this energy is exposed, it becomes a powerful tool the performer can use to build focus, momentum, and, most interestingly, more energy. Thus, when this natural energy is in play, the work becomes nearly effortless, physical challenges are abated, and focus is more uniform. For the street performer standing in the middle of the circle, invention will arise from the wellspring of this tapped, raw source of inspiration. They would become my model for a new life. I wanted the juice found in the jam. I wanted to run on natural energy.

Back with the Hat

The next day I placed a call to the number on the Hat's card and was directed by a woman with a gravelly voice to a place called the Pitch, a busker hangout on Queen Street. The Hat was indeed there and he quickly joined me. We took the one vacant table outside.

"Barnard opened this place especially for buskers, although anyone is welcome to drop a few coins," the Hat said as if we were continuing a conversation started a few moments ago. "This is the main hang for just about all of the guys. They all come here to talk shop, play chess or checkers, have a coffee, maybe light up a smoke."

Top Hat took off his hat and set it on the seat next to him.

"I take it you found the Rat Catcher and I presume you passed the test."

"I did and I thank you."

"Nothing any gentleman wouldn't do."

"And now I want to put it all together. And for that I

need the good counsel of a gentleman who has spent some time in the business world."

"Ah . . . that would be me."

"I am hoping you will help me clarify the applications to my work. I am already thinking of my life in sales as a life that is full of unexplored possibilities. So many things happen in any given day that I am sure there must be opportunities for new energy. Will you help me?"

"Go back to the issue that brought you here in the first place and let's start there."

"I came to England to grieve, because my mother loved it here. I was running out of energy at work. I sense that this journey is her legacy to me, and what I do with what I have learned will be my legacy to her. I don't understand it all, but it is what it is."

The Hat nodded. "Sometimes that is the best decision. Let things be and they will eventually speak to you and tell you the story."

"My approach to success from the day of my first sales call has been long hours, skipped vacations, more calls, more presentations, automated customer service, and short weekends. My problem is that my successful approach is burning me out, leaves no room for life, and doesn't seem to serve anyone very well."

"Your description tells me you obviously have achieved some clarity. What have you discovered?" the Hat asked.

"I have discovered that my life had become as ordinary as a street corner I might pass each day on the way to work. I barely noticed the array of changing details because it was the same corner. Then when I first started hanging out around you buskers, I actually felt misshapen, like I was this square hanging out with a bunch of triangles. I have a good job, work with some decent and talented people, and sell things that can make a difference in the quality of people's lives. But my heart wasn't in it, in the way a busker is present in the center of a circle.

"I saw how buskers dealt with hecklers determined to challenge the performer. And I saw performers treat the heckler like a jam and find the juice in the jam. I learned that a performer can deal with the heckler, you know, in a good way, and that it can generate even more energy. I realized we all deal with hecklers, and we can either let them destroy our energy or find a way to use their energy to build new possibilities!

"I will often be in the opening part of my presentation when one of the members of the committee assigned the task of evaluating my proposal will raise an objection or contentious issue. My approach has always been to mollify and move on as soon as possible with a lame comment about getting back to the issue later. I plan to explore ways to prepare for a deep exploration of the obvious issues so I can instead use that energy. I mean, that is what everyone is thinking about anyway, from the minute the issue is raised."

"I can see you have been doing a great deal of thinking. Let's talk some more. But first I need to avail myself of the facilities."

"Sure, Hat. I'll be here."

When the Hat returned, he suggested we take a walk so he could buy some socks.

"Why not? Let's walk."

"You know, Jim, in a way we are explorers. When you watch some of the truly great street performers, you get a sense that what they are doing has never happened before; it's new territory."

"Yes. That's it exactly."

"Jim, in a street performance there are bits and gags that have been part of the routine for years and years. In fact, any given show is really the sum of all the shows the performer has ever done. There isn't a lot of new material in any given show." He was smiling, like he was revealing a secret.

"Really. I was thinking that maybe I'd have to go back to my job and, you know, 'out with the old, in with the new.'"

"Not necessary. You see, the trick isn't to create new material all the time, though you always follow curiosity to find a new inspiration. The secret is to approach what you've done a million times with fresh thinking. If you have the right energy and approach to your work, you can make it as fresh as the first time, every time. When we no longer focus on the trick or the gag, and instead focus on the audience and the energy, it always seems fresh for them and for us. That way something done a thousand times is done for the first time. Pretty cool, huh?" the Hat replied.

"Hat, it is cool. So while my life may be full of the same content to be presented, my attitude is one of 'first time, every time.' I've learned that is the busker way, to see the uniqueness in each human encounter and embrace the new material that will always be generated in the circle. With that orientation, what seemed boring and repetitive to me is now full of novelty and it takes on a freshness. The words I use to describe the product benefits may be the same, but the human interactions will always provide me with novelty."

"Exactly. Here is the shoe store where I can get the pair of socks I need. Why don't you wait here in the afternoon sun? I'll be right back." And with that the Hat dashed into the store.

The Daydream

I found a sunlit spot on a small ledge that topped a wall extending from the side of the store. As I sat in the bright sunshine I began thinking about energy, and searching my mental photo album to find some examples. As my body warmed in the sunshine, I drifted into a semi-meditative state. An image of a shopping trip with Rebecca appeared in my mind's eye and I smiled.

After my first trip to England, Rebecca and I started to spend more time together. We found ourselves on a search for little hidden restaurants serving exotic food, and taking walks in parts of town we didn't know very well and generally being more adventurous and at times more amorous.

Though we were in our own city, life began to feel more like a vacation. I realized just how much energy and excitement I felt when I was around her.

One afternoon she said she wanted to buy a new pair of shoes. We already had a full night planned, and shopping for women's shoes was never one of my favorite activities, but in the spirit of new adventures, I acqui-esced to her request that I join her.

We stopped at several shoe stores, including a ware-house full of footwear, and some boutiques, each with beautiful displays of high-end footwear. I admit to be-ing a neophyte in the area of women's shoes, so the price tags of many of these shoes were a bit of a shock.

When I buy a pair of men's shoes, something that takes me fifteen minutes or less to do, I at least get a lot of leather, metal eyelets and soles, and simple practical-ity. In the women's shoe department, it seems the more expensive the shoe, the less of a shoe you actually get. One shoe with a couple of straps, each just a tad thicker than a piece of string, attached to a tiny piece of leather, had a $350 price tag.

We finally ended up at a family-run department store known for its selection of goods, free coffee, and gift wrapping. Rebecca doesn't really look for shoes; she's drawn to them.

Rebecca held my hand and made every attempt to pretend that she was still with me, though I could tell by the look in her eyes that she wanted to browse in a more Zen-like fashion, allowing each shoe to speak to her with-out the inconvenience of having to focus on me. Then we approached a large room in the back of the store with a sign above the entrance that said WOMEN'S SHOE CLEAR-ANCE. That was all it took. The room appeared to be full, floor to ceiling and wall to wall, of discontinued or deeply discounted shoes. Upon seeing this, Rebecca simply released my hand, and in a voice that sounded uncomfortably like that of a zombie, she said, "Ohh, I'm just going to peek in here to see . . . if . . . there . . . is . . . something . . . I . . . like." I went for a free cup of coffee.

There were a few chairs for men like me, and I decided to sit down and look through my Palm Pilot at messages from work, and perhaps write in my journal. When I sat, I noticed a large, fake pumpkin sitting next to the sales counter. At first I didn't think anything of it, but then realized that it was summer, and pumpkins generally don't make an appearance in the retail scene until fall. Upon further inspection, there were other smaller pumpkin objects set about the area, none with any indication that there was some kind of pumpkin-sponsored sale. I also noticed what looked like a small wooden chest, with gold hardware and shiny gold handles. It sat next to another small pumpkin. I tried to figure these things out, but soon found myself engaged in my work.

I'd been sitting for only a couple of minutes when I heard Rebecca burst into laughter. Rebecca has many laughs; some are forced, which she uses in social occasions when she's laughing at something that she doesn't really find funny, and a full-out, full-throated belly laugh that bursts out of her, real and infectious. I looked up to see her standing with a lanky kid wearing a loud tie, rumpled shirt, and pants that hung low and covered his shoes. He was also wearing a purple hat with gold trim.

A little later I heard Rebecca laughing again, this time with the sound of happy surprise. When I looked up, I couldn't see her, but I could see the sales kid, still wearing the hat. Curiosity got the best of me and I decided to investigate the situation.

When I came into the room, Rebecca waved emphatically to me to take a seat next to hers. "He's great!" she said, leaning right into me when I sat. "He's hysterical."

"Who? The kid in the goofy hat?" I asked, wondering what he could be doing that would delight Rebecca so.

"Yes. He's not goofy, he's . . . oh wait, just wait." The kid was on his way over again. He carefully knelt down before me.

"Sir, I have waited for you, I would like your permission, though I know none is needed, to attempt to find, out of all these shoes, the one destined to belong to this fine young woman."

I looked at Rebecca. "Is he serious?" I asked. Rebecca laughed again.

"Sure, whatever does it for you," I said, being smart-alecky. I sensed this could be fun. He was in his mid-twenties with a kind of nerdy look to him, with wavy brown hair and a distinctly formal approach. His name tag only had the initials THP written across it. And given my journey I was more than a little bit interested in his sales approach.

"My lady, I beg your patience, but I have found these boxes, each of which contain not just a shoe, but a new life, a new look, a new possibility. Mayhap you would allow me to see if these shoes have finally found the one woman who would but fulfill their destiny, indeed your destiny?" he said with seriousness.

"You want to what?" Rebecca could hardly speak, she was laughing so hard.

"I got some shoes here, wanna try them on?" he said, breaking character and making the whole exchange very funny and engaging. "Huh?"

"Oh yes, but I think I like the Prince Charming routine better," Rebecca proclaimed.

"Certainly. I will now take my leave; when I return we shall discover if you've finally come back to the right place." At that point he headed over to grab the small treasure chest, which he then carried over and set it on the floor next to Rebecca's now bare feet.

As he was doing this, a few other female customers had become amused at what he was doing, curious about the box and his purple, floppy hat. He pulled a small shoe store footstool over in front of Rebecca, and then opened the treasure chest, carefully concealing the contents. His face seemed to glow when out of the box appeared a small, purple velvet pillow. It was festooned with gold rope trim and fancy tassels. As he took the pillow out, he held it up for the other women to see. He carefully checked the pillow for lint or other debris, plucking and brushing the surface of the pillow, making its surface clean and without distraction. He set the pillow onto the stool, fluffing it into perfection.

Rebecca squealed with glee.

"My ladies, I beg you all to be of good cheer, for there are many shoes that must find a foot before midnight!" His delivery wasn't sappy or performed; it was in a matter-of-fact tone that made the whole thing tongue in cheek. Rebecca didn't mind; she was in shoe paradise.

THP took out a pair of shoes and, resting Rebecca's foot on the purple pillow, he slowly tried to slip the shoe on her foot. This wasn't your usual does-that-fit shoe sales approach; it was more skilled, more interesting, and certainly more entertaining.

The first two pairs of shoes didn't fit, and he apologized for the obvious disappointment. Finally, he arrived at a pair of shoes that came in a bloodred box. He pulled out a small black shoe with a thin high heel. He carefully looked at the shoe, smiled, nodded his head, and slowly slipped the shoe on Rebecca's tiny foot. It fit perfectly.

"Ohh, I think these are great . . . these are really cute," she said.

THP pushed his stool out of the way and knelt down on one knee. "I have finally found the only woman who would fit such exquisite shoes. It has been a long wait, and many have tried, but these clearly belong to you."

He took off his floppy hat in mock respect and Rebecca laughed and clapped.

Rebecca decided to try on many more shoes in the next half hour and each time THP would commend her for "returning" and trying on more shoes. He jumped to other women, each getting a personal version of his unusual style.

When we were ready to check out I asked about the name tag and all the pumpkins.

"Sir, my name is a secret, just call me T.P. if you wish. The pumpkins are just a reminder that at midnight, the coach turns to a pumpkin, and the lady drops her slipper. It is my job to find her, for all these shoes are slippers dropped behind. These all belong to someone, and I get to find out who that someone is," he explained with both wit and seriousness. He continued, "The slipper is dropped at a celebration, a dance. I'm here to remind my customers that the right shoe on a lady's foot returns her to the scene of the crime, to the celebration that she wants to get back to."

"You're something else. I'm buying more than I planned to buy," Rebecca said. "A lot more!" She was.

When he handed Rebecca the credit receipt, he walked around the counter and handed it her. "Thank you and Godspeed," he said, after which he turned back to help another woman waiting for the purple pillow.

At the time, it was simply an interesting adventure. Now I realized that what I had seen was a young sales associate using the principles I had learned from the Rat Catcher and Top Hat. His pitch was the shoe store and his role was a prince. There was a jam every time he placed a shoe on a foot. His mess contained mostly shoes and he handled them in such a way that one's curiosity was tweaked. He had an abundance of props for insurance. The close was well orchestrated with the perfect fit. The circle he established assured future sales from the interested and curious. I am sure some of what he did had been done before, but it always felt like the first time. And the hat was full when we left. It all fell into place for me now that I had the language.

"Jim."

"Bartholomew James!"

I looked up to see the Hat standing in front of me with a small package. "You found your socks?"

"Indeed. Where were you just now?"

I told him and Top Hat delighted in the Cinderella story and the way T.P. seemed to bridge sales associate and street performer.

"Why do you suppose you remembered that incident?"

"It is an application of the language of natural energy in a retail setting. Not my kind of sales, but sales nevertheless."

"You will find all the applications you need, Jim. Your mind is already working the problem."

"Yes, it is. What a great time for the two of us to get down to specifics for the pharmaceutical industry."

"No."

"Excuse me?"

"I must now take my leave."

"Why?"

"You are well on your way, Jim, and right now the gentlemanly thing to do is leave you to the rest of your journey of discovery. You are ready and you have learned our language, and the language will help you think like a street performer. It is time for you to go back and put into practice all you have learned. You will make mistakes and those mistakes will be a catalyst for your learning. You will develop and refine the language of natural energy to fit your needs. That is how it must be. I will leave you with two things. But first, do you have something for me?"

A Final Envelope

I looked confused, but recovered quickly. "Oh boy."
And I reached in my back pocket and pulled out
the same envelope I had received from Top Hat some
weeks earlier. It was even worse for wear but still sealed.

"I will take that for my collection, putting it in a
place of honor, and I will give you this." Top Hat re-
moved a large envelope from his inside jacket pocket
and handed it to me. "This is an envelope that can only
be opened when you are absolutely sure of your commitment to apply to your work the language of energy
and the other things you have learned by hanging with
buskers. That commitment can be summarized in a few
words and you might want to write them down."

I pulled out my journal and began to take notes as
the Hat spoke.

"When you open the envelope, you are committing
to a life fueled from the inside out with natural energy.
Follow the instructions on the inside and you will be
guaranteed success in whatever you do. You will be a top

performer for life." The Hat smiled. "And just in case you didn't get that all down, there is a copy inside and you can review it once you make a commitment to natural energy."

I quickly finished writing in my book and looked up to make a comment. But the Hat was no longer there. In the crowd on the street I saw a gentleman, hat bobbing as he walked away. Then for a moment the hat came off and was held high in one hand, waving.

Good-bye and thanks again, Top Hat, I thought. *I see the rest is up to me. And considering the key ingredient of my future success is natural energy, that is how it should be.*

I returned to the hotel and after setting out my writing material, journal, and other notes on the desk and after preparing a pot of tea, I got to work. I was determined to organize what I had learned before my flight the next morning and it was well into the night before I finished my personal summary of the language of energy. The last thing I did was to prepare a notecard to use as a quick reminder.

The Language of Energy

Claim Your Pitch

Juice the Jam

Mine the Mess

Develop Insurance

Choose a Close

Pass the Hat

Build a Circle

PART FIVE
TOP PERFORMER
AT WORK

Back to Reality

I was very aware of the envelope that I carried as I went through security at Boston's Logan Airport. Perhaps it was the question I was asked at Heathrow that caused me to be so conscious of the envelope. The agent had said:

"Are you carrying anything given to you by a stranger?"

Since the Hat was not a stranger I could have said no, but being a total straight shooter I had taken out the envelope and said, "Only this, sir, but it is from a friend." The agent had smiled and sent me on my way, probably musing about the odd people you meet in life.

Rebecca was in a holding pattern outside the airport and my phone call released her. She arrived at the curb shortly after I did and we quickly greeted and were on our way.

I began telling Rebecca about my plans, and I felt my enthusiasm build as I talked. When we finally arrived at my townhouse, I felt none of the usual jet lag. I was on fire.

Rebecca looked at me when the car came to a stop. "I have never seen you like this, Jim. There is no question in my mind you have found what you were looking for. I just want to know what it is."

I smiled at her. "You are going to be the first to know and, for a little while, the only one to know."

We ordered takeout and talked for hours about energy and the language that releases it. I told Rebecca that I had a different strategy to communicate with my colleagues from the one I used the last time. That's what I meant about her being the only one to know for a while, a reference to my new strategy. I had decided to let my actions at work speak first, and if it all went well and if I had good results, well, then the energy was more likely to be natural. And when I arrived at work the next day, I stuck to my plans.

Rather than talk about the Rat Catcher, the Hat, and my amazing journey, I went right to work. People would ask me politely about my trip and I would simply say it was great and it was good to be back at work. I felt alive and also peaceful.

Other than Rebecca, the only one I went into detail with was Mia. To Mia I had said, "I am going to use the language of energy in my own work, and if I am successful, others will ask me what I am doing and that will be a great example of natural energy. If no one sees a difference, then there is nothing to talk about." And I set about doing exactly that.

As a symbol of my new direction, I wore a backpack and left the briefcase at home. I would put unusual things in the pack. One day I was trying to gauge the interest a client had in placing an order and I took out a tape measure, a rain gauge, and a contract. "I wonder if I might get a measure of your interest, sir?" My conversation with the potential client took on a lightness and authenticity after that.

I put away my extensively detailed Rolodex containing carefully collected information about my prospects; their hobbies, pets, kids, favorite sports team, and car, and simply adopted a curious attitude about all the people I met. My curiosity led to a deeper listening that felt calm, and I no longer felt the anxiety I had always felt when I was with an important client. I considered my presentations and meetings opportunities to connect with other human beings and to discover interesting things about them, their points of view, tastes, and preferences. This discovery approach always seemed to generate energy and I enjoyed becoming a student of life. I looked at each person as a teacher and the more I listened the more I learned.

It felt uncomfortable at first, because anytime we change a pattern or redesign our thinking and routines, we leave behind the security of known territory. I was a creature of habit, like so many of us, and habits help us manage the chaos by making it more predictable. Now, as I leaned into my discomfort and spent my days trying new things, new approaches, new language, I felt a wellspring of energy wash over me. Even when I was doing the most routine of tasks I would challenge myself to do something different and create the energy of the first time.

I stopped filling out reports at my desk, as I had to do for years, and decided to pick it all up and take it to the Galleria Mall, sit in the courtyard with a cup of coffee, and do them there. I got them done in the usual amount of time and had more energy along the way.

I was extremely conscious of claiming my pitch. In a conference where I was one of many presentations, I wanted to do something special to claim my pitch, something unique. So I came to the ballroom where the event was going to happen before anyone arrived and took pictures of the empty room and transferred them to my PowerPoint. Then when it was my turn to present, I said, "Welcome. The picture you see is this room with no one present. But now it is full of energy and interest. You are the energy and when you fill this room, you bring that energy to an empty space. I am here to serve the energy and compassion that is already present, not to replace it."

In my group presentations to medical centers, I chose to insert a few slides of animals and nature in my Power-Point, which gave me an opportunity to talk with my audience about subjects where everyone could chime in. Later, I spontaneously acted out the functions of a healthy liver and explained why our new drug restored that balance when the liver was diseased. It was a bit cumbersome but full of laughs and they complimented me on the most enjoyable presentation. I also received an order.

One day I'd heard that the Norwegian head nurse at Bloomington Medical was going to retire. I hired a friend of mine who was accomplished at playing classical guitar. My friend sat in the lobby and softly played Norwegian folk tunes. It changed the mood of the whole complex and started a conversation that led to an invitation for my friend to play his guitar weekly at the center. It also showed everyone at Bloomington that I really knew and cared about them.

On another occasion I spilled coffee on my white shirt while sitting in the café with a prospect. In the back of my mind I heard the words, "It's all material, juice the jam." Without missing a beat, I used the outline of the coffee stain to discuss a molecule that was important in the success of one of our drugs.

When my overhead projector emitted a puff of smoke and went black, I knew it was more than a bulb. On the spot I decided to tell stories as a substitute and while my presentation was less visual, it was more real and connected.

As my insurance grew, so did my assurance, and I never found myself without a tried-and-true idea for those times when such were needed.

On entering a room full of doctors who were to be my pitch, I decided that sitting at the head of the table was a bit much, and I changed the pitch by saying, "I want to sit in the middle of the table as a physical representation of how we work in partnership. We also hold physicians in high esteem, so it is only right that a physician sit at the head of the table." It had always been the way I felt, and my words carried an authentic tone. The interaction that followed had none of the usual stiffness.

This became insurance and I never sat at the head of the table again.

On another occasion I decided to breathe some life into a part of the process that was usually dead. Wrapping up the details of the service agreement took a great deal of time and was somewhat boring, so I arranged for a small lunch to be served at the end of the process, creating a more energetic finish.

My hat began to fill with new orders, letters to the company, kind comments, and the new energy I felt for my work. I became an increasingly creative closer and often used the closing of a door and the crossing of a threshold as a visual example that joined my request for the business.

At the end of the day Rebecca and I would exchange notes. She was on fire, as well. From the very beginning of her career as a customer service trainer she had carried a belief that her training needed to be of the highest professional standard, so she was tightly scripted to be sure the presentation was polished and complete in every way. Her handouts were flawless and her overheads polished. Every session ran, quite literally, like clockwork, for they varied little until the Q&A. Then one day a waiter entered the room while she was explaining a difficult concept and began noisily pouring water in the water pitchers. She stopped her presentation and admonished him, waiting until he left the room to resume her presentation. The audience turned cold and uninterested. It was a struggle to finish, because she knew something was wrong. After the session, her sponsor in a clipped tone told her that the water was requested and that the waiter was a favorite of everyone in the facility. She was devastated.

When she shared this with me, I asked her what she might have done differently. She thought of the language of energy and responded, "Juice the jam."

It was a week later during a presentation to a stiff and emotionless group of participants that something similar happened. The buffet table was at the back of the room and two of the waitstaff began setting it up for lunch a full hour early. She felt herself tense up and then, just as quickly, relax. She walked to the back of the room commenting on how each of us is served daily in many ways by people who are usually behind the scenes and that we have an obligation to recognize these people and thank them. She introduced each of them and they received a loud ovation. She then interviewed them about lunch and demonstrated proper use of a buffet table. The distraction was defused and she had the full attention of the group for the first time. She had juiced the jam and created a stronger circle.

Everywhere I looked I would see my own version of the pitch, jam, mess, insurance, hat, close, and circle and I would make notes in the evening. My results improved but, more importantly, I once again enjoyed my work. I was alive. Then out of the blue something special happened.

The Next Step

I was working on a project one night when the phone rang. "Jim, I don't know if you know me, but I'm a second-year guy at Jensen and have recently been assigned to Mia. I want to talk with you about your approach. I really think I could learn a great deal from you, and Mia has agreed to let me ask. She did not know whether you would have the time or not, but I wanted to call."

"What is your name?"

"J.C."

"I know you, J.C. You were the first second-year Golden Eagle in the history of the company. What on earth do you want from me?"

"I want to learn your secrets."

"What makes you think I have any secrets?" I asked.

"Didn't you study street performers in England and Ireland?"

"I am not sure 'study' is the right word, but I certainly learned a great deal from them."

"When I was twelve and we needed extra money in the family I went to the local grocery store and sat on the steps and played a bad clarinet. I would leave the case open in front of me and there would always be a couple dollars there an hour later. Then I discovered that talking to people and engaging them in fun ways would make the time pass more quickly. After that the amount of money in my case grew. And during a difficult year in our family's life, I was able to make a real monetary contribution. I always felt I had learned something important, but I could never frame what I learned. That is what I want to learn from you."

"I'll give it some thought, J.C. Why don't you call me in a couple days?"

"I could come over right now."

"Got too much on my plate, J.C. Call me in a couple."

The Commitment

"Who was that, Jim?" Rebecca asked me.

"A guy from work."

"Really. What did he want?"

I told her the story.

"And what are you going to do?"

"I don't know, Rebecca. Maybe see how much he really wants to learn. Put him off for a while. But I have a decision to make." And I told her about the second envelope and about the role of commitment.

"So you were told not to open the envelope until you were sure you were ready to make a real commitment. It seems to me you've made that commitment."

"I've been exploring the language and laws of natural energy for three months. Is that a commitment? Perhaps. But working with another agent is a commitment that can't be taken lightly," I said. Rebecca just smiled.

"What?" I asked.

"And the Hat told you that the envelope contains all you need to be successful for the long run?"

"Something like that."

"And?"

"And I think I will open the envelope."

The Contents of the Envelope

"Are you nervous, Jim?"

"A little."

Inside the envelope was a letter. It had a circle with a dot inside it and one sentence:

Now do for others what has been done for you.

We just sat for a while thinking of the enormity of the challenge. Then I looked at Rebecca and said, "Brilliant. By becoming a teacher I will receive the energy that comes from serving others and my commitment can only grow. Have I told you about J.C.? I think he may be getting close to becoming my first assignment." And I filled her in on J.C.

After a number of intentional delays and a few well-placed hurdles, it became clear to me that J.C. was indeed motivated by more than a passing fancy, and that he was ready for the next step. I asked J.C. to meet me for lunch and the cycle that started in London began to repeat itself.

The Bee

I waited near the pulpit and watched the woman I loved deeply come down the aisle on her father's arm. High overhead I heard a faint buzzing sound. I glanced up to see a small bee circling in the reflected light of the stained-glass windows.

Hello, Mom. Thanks for coming.

EPILOGUE
From Carr Hagerman, PSP

I t had been raining for days, perhaps weeks. The lifeless clouds seemed tethered into place and never moved, so the rain came straight down. The cobblestone streets were nearly frozen, and few people dared to venture out, leaving the city eerily bereft of human activity. The bubonic plague had turned the city hallow and deadly.

The year was 1347, and the black plague was killing one in three Europeans. The rain couldn't wash away the disease; the plague came from the holds of ships on the backs of infected rats; their fleas spread the disease on food, blankets, brushes, cargo, and even medical equipment. And in this way the disease easily spread until Europe was engulfed in the worst epidemic in human history. It was a dark passage for the planet.

Often the darkest of times spawn the best in human innovation and invention. In medieval Europe, it was the entrepreneur as well as the scientist who ended the plague.

The Rat Catcher was an entrepreneur, his occupation born out of necessity and opportunity. The Rat Catcher would go house-to-house, town-to-town, and city-to-city and, for a fee, exterminate the disease-carrying rodents. It was a dangerous occupation, but one that offered rewards in the form of income and saved human lives.

I was seventeen years old when I first saw a copy of Rembrandt's etching of a rat catcher dated 1632. The tiny picture depicts a man in rags carrying rat pelts and a cage of cats, about ready to enter a home to rid it of its diseased vermin. The etching is a hopeful rendering of life at a time when so many lived in fear of the disease, and there was little hope.

In what is one of those extraordinary coincidences in life, years prior to seeing Rembrandt's snapshot of medieval life, I had created a street character of my own who I named Rat Catcher.

In the summer of 1977, I first transformed myself into a roving street character at a renaissance festival in Shakopee, Minnesota. I wore rags and covered myself with dirty makeup, wore a strange hat, and carried a big stick. The Rat Catcher also carried a nasty countenance, and dug under tree, bush, and bench in a vain search for rats. The character was a big hit with audiences and became a staple at the festival for thirty years. The Rat Catcher also traveled to other festivals around the U.S., where he was always received with enthusiasm. During much of that time I was Rat Catcher on the weekends and a professional businessperson during the week.

I had never seen this Rembrandt work before I created my performance, but when I did see it I realized that my character and the one captured in the little drawing were nearly identical. At some level, I felt connected to this man and his job.

Over the years I have formed a theory about what we rat catchers do and something we now call "natural energy." The medieval rat catcher, like any entrepreneur, discovered natural energy in the necessity of his tasks. Opportunity is often born out of such events, and an entrepreneur senses the energy of that opportunity and captures or creates an innovative response. My Rat Catcher wasn't responding to skyrocketing death rates and neighborhood fears like my medieval model, but I discovered the energy in the curiosity of crowds. For me, the opportunity was to tap into the embedded desire of the audience to laugh and be entertained. Rembrandt's ragged exterminator saved lives by killing rats. I relieved the burdens of life by releasing laughter.

No matter how you see it, natural energy lives at the crossroads of opportunity and curiosity. That is the impetus for the journey of our protagonist; I hope it will be yours, too.

ACKNOWLEDGMENTS

We would like to thank those who supported this effort.

First and foremost is Will Schwalbe, editor in chief of Hyperion. This is Steve's fifth book with Will, and each engagement has more magic than the one before. Will, you are incredible and the team at Hyperion is outstanding. That team includes Bob Miller, Ellen Archer, Jane Comins, Emily Gould, Sarah Schaffer, and Phil Rose.

We would like to acknowledge the continued great work of Margret McBride and her group at McBride Literary Agency. That group includes Margret McBride, Donna DeGutis, Faye Atchison, and Anne Bomke.

And we would like to thank those who have read drafts of the manuscript, made contributions, seen clearly what we are doing, and in some way have joined or supported the effort: Shawn Hunter, Paul Sanders, Mick Lundzer, Deena Ebert, Kris Brooks, Patrick North, and Tena Crawford.

Steve's individual acknowledgments include:

While Will Schwalbe is first among professionals and friends in his contributions, Janell, my wife, is first in my life. Her unflagging support and positive attitude have helped me sustain the writer's commitment in the darkest and the busiest of times. I love and cherish you, Janell.

My daughters have been and continue to be the source of much of my energy. Beth, who died so young and who joins me every time I speak. I work on leaving a legacy worthy of her. Melissa, who has the gift of words and who continues to be one of the world's great mothers as she raises two beautiful daughters, Madeleine and Mia, with her dashing and brilliant husband, Paul. Melanie, my youngest daughter, who is such a positive force in the world and who is about to make her mark in the medical profession seventy years after my mother first made hers. And Karen, the daughter I didn't know existed until she called one day after twenty years of searching.

Finally, my sister Barbara, the saint, who with her husband, Larry, and daughter, Zhu Zhu, took Dad and Mom into their home, where they both thrived and where my dad, Carl, still lives comfortably, surrounded by loving family.

And then there is my co-author, Carr. I have attempted to work collaboratively before and for the most part it just didn't work. I began to wonder if true collaboration was even possible or if there was something faulty in me. This time was delightfully different. As

I read this manuscript, I am unable to tell who wrote what, for our contributions are so completely integrated. What a neat experience!

Carr's individual acknowledgments include:

Steve Lundin, who brought the poet's heart to this work and to our friendship and has opened my life to new ways of thinking and creating. We should all be so lucky to have such loving and talented colleagues.

John Christensen, whose bright imagination and friendship opened up new possibilities.

Crist Ballas, who inspires me.

Patty Griffin and Tony Stebley for their counsel, humor, intellectual challenge, and for being so damn supportive.

Mick Lunzer for bringing such great energy to this project.

My brother John, who encouraged me to embrace life's experience as a map for my writing.

My father for getting it right.

And Marian Tenold, who has been an anchor of tenderness, patience, and loving-kindness that made it all possible.

I dedicate my work to Penn and Teller, the buskers of Covent Garden, and the cast of the MN Rennaissance Festival.

Dogs rule!

To contact or book Steve or Carr for your event, simply contact Top Performer Academy.

Top Performer Academy has been established to develop Top Performers in organizations. The Academy offers an opportunity for a business leader to participate in an acclaimed business management process called Blueprint for Excellence in order to establish an important foundation of goals, priorities, and metrics. This is usually done in groups of ten, comprised of leaders from noncompeting businesses. More than 500 firms have used Blueprint for Excellence effectively.

Supplementing the Blueprint for Excellence is an ongoing series of stimulating educational modules designed by the author of *FISH!*, *FISH! Sticks*, *FISH! for Life*, *CATS: The Nine Levels of Innovation*, and *Top Performer*, Stephen Lundin (Big Tuna, Ph.D.). These modules developed by this writer, filmmaker, entrepreneur, and former business school dean will provoke you and your group of peers to engage in topics clearly connected to top performance.

Chapters are being formed around the globe. Please use the contact information below to identify the chapter nearest you.

Top Performer Academy
335 North Last Chance Gulch
Helena, Montana 59624
406-449-5559
info@topperformer.com

To learn more, visit the Top Performer Web site:
www.topperformer.com